Daffodil
A Mother's Journey

DAFFODIL

A Mother's Journey

by
DeMetria Hayes
Cover Design by Charisma Stirgus

Grace Under Fire Publishing
Durham, North Carolina

DAFFODIL: Mother's Journey

Grace Under Fire Publishing
Post Office 100 Glen Falls Ln Suite 202
Durham, NC 27713

E-mail:**daffodil@demetriahayes.com**
Web:**demetriahayes.com**
Speaking Engagements
Bulk Purchases

This book in its entirety is true, but most if the names have been changed to protect the privacy of the people mentioned.

All Scripture quotations, unless otherwise noted, are taken from the *Holy Bible: New International Online Version, (NIV) Gateway). Copyright 1973, 1978, 1984, 2011 by Biblica Inc. All rights reserved worldwide.*

Copyeditor: **Tina Winograd**
Cover Designer: **Charisma Stirgus**

A Journey with a Purpose

This book is dedicated to my strong and beautiful daughter Charisma Stirgus: Our colorful journey has provided me with the knowledge, experience, and courage to confront adversity. You are an extension of me and I am honored to be your mother. The strength of our relationship now shows a keen awareness of God's unchanging hand. The purpose of our lives may no be to our understanding, but to God be the glory.

I pray your journey through life brings you joy, peace, happiness, and understanding. I encourage you to build on and develop those characteristics that are the foundation for the dynamic woman you desire to become.

I encourage you to pull from your well of positivity, sincerity, and kind-heartedness you have roasting at the core of your soul. Use the God given power to soar beyond what the eye can see.

I want to broaden this dedication to mothers and daughters everywhere. Do not let your current situation with your mother tarnish your future. Reposition yourself and let your light shine. It will take you on a journey to build character, confidence, and faith. Most importantly, listen to the inner audible voice of God declaring his Love for you.

Life is a journey and a journey deserves a journal. Cultivate every moment. It's worth your time.

CONTENTS

Foreword

Freedom, forgiveness, and the will to fight are extraordinary life experiences shared in Daffodil. While these three words are common in our vocabulary, their manifestation and actualization are often choked in the tangled lives we secretly live.

Our freedom to love and to be loved can become beaten down by past pains, and stifled by present insecurities. Our inabilities to forgive and release ourselves keep us hostage to people, places and things that cloud our vision, leaving us with the darkness of hate and regret. The fight to survive is often lost and strangled because we are too afraid to confront our shame.

In this book, Demetria Hayes invites you on the courageous journey of her own transformation. A transformation only realized by running, walking, and sometimes crawling through her experiences to Freedom, Forgiveness and the Will to Fight.

She allows us to see the pain of a terrified, self-doubting mother trying to relate to a detached and withdrawn daughter. We feel the shame of a battered wife trying to survive the abusive marriage. While her story is riveting and sometimes shocking, Demetria doesn't tell her story for pity or to incur your sorrow. She tells her story to speak life to your Daffodil.

The Daffodil is synonymous with Spring. It symbolizes the end of winter giving to new birth, new beginnings. Demetria's battle with Freedom, Forgiveness and her will to Fight were almost lost forever. Harsh storms impeded her ability to bloom…to become…to fly. Like many delicate and beautiful flowers, it appeared her Daffodil was crushed and stomped, unable to survive the tempest of her life. But in reality, its bulb was hidden in the ground, protected by soil and covered by a force she couldn't see. And when time had passed, and the prison of the defeating storm lifted, the leaves of the Daffodil begin to bloom…to become… to take wing.

The bondage of violence and insecurities will end, and you will say, like this phenomenal author, "I am not a prisoner anymore, but today… I soar.

-Lady Suzette Spence
Elect Lady of Word Empowerment. Durham, NC

Preface

This book is not intended to make anyone look or feel bad, but bring to light that abuse is prevalent when you least expect it.

I initially started writing solely to reach out to my daughter, to give her understanding of why our relationship suffered and ask for her forgiveness. As I wrote to my daughter, it developed into much more than I anticipated.

While going through this self-reflection I experienced shameful loneliness and embarrassment. However, I know beyond a shadow of a doubt there is a supreme purpose for my life. I feel God directed me to write this not to have people feel sorry for me or put my life on display, but to help those suffering at the hands of oneself or others.

God has allowed me to hear countless stories about abusive relationships others suffer to help me see this book is needed. At times thinking back on events, most were painful to write, by no means did I include everything.

After giving a battered woman syndrome presentation at WE church in Durham, North Carolina, God ministered to my heart and released me from the shame, embarrassment and the fear of being judged and the thought of others seeing me as damaged goods.

Un-forgiveness is a powerful weapon. It can steal, kill or destroy one's internal being but being able to forgive myself showed me how forgiveness can restore, empower, uplift and set free. The curse cannot be broken until the curse is known. Deuteronomy 28.

Daffodil may be hard to read for some. It will take you on a journey through happiness, sadness, and loss, even violence but bring you to a place of healing, joy and peace. I want all to know I am a survivor and I've been made whole.

My desire is to provide the tools needed to heal, educate, and empower women to know their self-worth is worth preserving and well deserved. Let's break the silence of domestic violence!

DAFFODIL

Chapter 1
Explosive

The brutal attacks by my husband mentally toured and parlayed me. Out of nowhere he clenched his knuckles, a solid blow to my face threw me back. My head was throbbing and spinning so fast I couldn't remember where I was or how I got there. I remember sitting for hours hidden in the closet pretending to be someplace else.

Each day I would suffer some form of abuse. It started to feel more like a dream but it wasn't it was real. I couldn't afford to feel the full range of feelings in my body while being abused.

The pain was so great I learned to suppress my feelings and wished I were dead. I couldn't see away out. It was easier to pretend I was the Queen of England or the First Lady than to acknowledge the horror I was experiencing. I tried to bury it in my mind by shutting down any love I had and went numb for years.

The years were tough and the pain, outrage, hate, vengeance and confusion from my marriage took its toll on my relationship with my little girl. I needed to forgive myself from past hurts and pain, and forgive my husband in order to ask my daughter's forgiveness.

After stumbling upon an English paper my daughter Jade wrote in college titled, "My Relationship with Mom," my heart exploded. My eyes opened to what I could not hear during her school age years.

The following insert of her paper will touch your heart.

My Relationship with Mom

My mom and I have gone through a lot over the years. My entire childhood we never got along. I couldn't stand her. The thing that bothered me the most was the fact we could never talk to each other, not without arguing. We'd end up going at it every time I wanted to talk to her.

For us there was no sitting down and having a normal conversation. I used to think it was a Detroit kind of problem. Mothers and daughters don't have normal conversations in Detroit because we are on the northwest side and all the streets have Indian names like Chippewa, Pembroke, and Mendota. We live on sacred Indian burial ground. Cursed! But why *us* and not the other mothers and daughters I see here? I started realizing Detroit had nothing to do with it.

Don't get me wrong, I love my mom; but our eyes could never see each other. I felt like she was blind when it came to me. I felt like they always have been. She paid more attention to everyone else than she did to me. She was always telling me, "Jade you need to grow up." But how could that happen when I felt like she was always treating me like a child?

I wish I knew the reason we never got along; why it was never easy for us; why our relationship as far as I remember has been explosive at times, but mostly a silent battlefield. And that's the crazy part: that silence.

Back in my early elementary years, she was cool. We were best friends. But by the time I was in fifth grade, for no reason, she'd flip on me. I think how much easier it would have been to have built something with her when I was younger. But that didn't happen, and you can't make things happen when they never did.

When I was in middle school, she used to go through all of my clothes. I'd come home and find the ones she didn't like me wearing were gone. She'd take them and hold them up in her room: some shirts, but mostly my jeans. My jeans were the most noticeable because I never had a lot of clothes. I really didn't.

What really got me was when I'd go to her room and there they would be in her closet, under her bed, and behind it. And when I'd ask her about it, she'd deny it and give me a look. I called that look the `blankness' because it was like a mask; a`blankness' hides the truth with a smile kind of look. But it was all still just `blankness' to me.

In order to get through what I was going through-the loneliness I felt at home-I became the class clown at school. I was always getting into fights and staying in some type of trouble. I became bitter, mean, and to some a bully. Not a lot of people knew about that.

After the principal's office called me down three times in one week, I had to ask myself why I was constantly getting into trouble. Was I crying out for attention or taking my frustration with our problems out on everybody else? I was young, but those were the questions I never asked aloud.

I felt like my little brothers hated me. And I got it. They called me The Punisher because of my mental and physical torture. I choked, slapped, slammed, and antagonized them until they got mad. And then I'd beat them up. In their words, I was a super bully.

Things didn't start getting better until my junior year in high school. I wanted to change and become closer to my mother, but whenever I'd tell her anything, she'd tell someone else. I'd always find out because whenever she would tell my aunts anything they'd come back and tell me. They would give me a report. How could anybody not be done with her after that? I felt like I could never tell her anything again.

My aunts started hearing from me all the time; started knowing me more than she ever did. I remember noticing she felt that, how I had stopped coming to her. I could see she didn't like it. I could see it in her `blankness.' It had a paralyzing, crippling effect on her. And I was hurt so I didn't mind sharing the pain. Seeing me able to express myself to someone else the way I should be able to talk to her, I'm not going to lie, I liked it.

I started to notice this thing works both ways. She didn't know me and to me she was a stranger. I was young, so for me it was all about getting even, but I still needed to know who my mother was. I needed to find out what was behind the mask because it killed me inside to know that every day, for my mother, was Halloween.

One day I found out my mom had gone through all of my things and I started thinking it was my turn. I waited until she left and I went into her room. I went through her drawers, under her bed, everywhere I could, looking for answers. And in her closet, I found some. Who knew the answers I'd find would get me to a place where I would start questioning myself. How could I have known that?

My Journey

Over the years, in my own way, I tried to reach out to my daughter, but my attempts never quite connected in the way she needed. She wanted answers, so she went looking for them in my diary hidden in the closet. Every night she read intensely, hoping to get some understanding of our estranged relationship.

Through the development of this book, I discovered a way to connect with my daughter and give her the answers in a way that expresses my unconditional love. This is a mother's journey to find a release of peace through darkness to light.

The following pages are a collection my own diary entries of what life was like while raising her. Along with personal letters and poems, they tell a story.

Chapter 2
Meet Klyde Stealar

My path to growing up and motherhood came at a fairly young age. I took my own route and the results were not what I expected. When I was younger, I dreamed of a fairytale life and what my perfect husband would be like.

After high school, I reached the next chapter in my life where I was in pursuit to discover myself, but I needed a job. So I searched the classifieds, applied at Creative Concepts and got hired on the spot

Wayne and Michelle, a husband and wife team, rented office space on the third floor of the Crossroads Office Centre between Southfield Freeway & The Lodge. It was a wholesale company who sold designer perfume in off-brand packaging, door to door. My job was to convince people my perfume was the real thing, but packaged in off brand packing (hard sale).

Creative Concepts was a business casual workplace. Most men wore a suit and tie. One day a medium height, brown skinned, slew footed guy walked through the office doors. He reminded me of the comedian Martin Lawrence, but slightly shorter. He had long slender fingers, neatly manicured and polished nails, and his left pinky nail was long enough to scoop a cup of ice cream. His clothes were neat and clean. He wore a blue jean outfit, Adidas gym shoes, and a blue jean bebop cap.

He definitely turned heads, not because he looked so good, but because he stood out like a sore thumb. He turned around and I noticed one gold plated tooth in the front of his mouth. He walked in with confidence. He attracted attention. The women started chattering.

Everyone was intrigued by this mysterious person and so was I. Wayne introduced him as Klyde Stealer. When he spoke, his dialect was unfamiliar. His words were almost unrecognizable because I couldn't understand what language he was speaking. I had never heard anyone speak that way. It was not at all like a Michigander.

In the office, every day was like a pep rally. Wayne pumped us up with a motivational speech to go out and sell. He'd yell, "Let's get fired up. It's hump day! Sell, sell, sell!" The room was always full of adrenaline. I started off as a salesperson but worked my way up to an outside sales manager in no time. I had a team of people under me. We canvased businesses only. Each team was assigned a territory. We even went on road trips to places like South Bend, Indiana and Toledo, Ohio.

One day, after the pump up power rally, Wayne assigned Klyde to my team. I gave Klyde a couple of territories we could work together. I asked him if he was familiar with the 6 Mile and Southfield area. He was, so we started there.

Since, this was his first time in the field, I thought we should work together as a team, but he walked ahead of me. After several hours, neither of us sold a bottle of perfume. We were both disappointed. I didn't want him to stop working at Creative Concepts. "Let's take a break," I said. Since I wasn't familiar with the neighborhood Klyde suggested the movies.

We went to the Mercury Theater next door to Wrigley's supermarket. The Mercury was not big and a little outdated, but the murals painted on the walls and ceiling amazed me. The colors were bright and inviting. By the time, the movie ended we had just enough time to report back to work. From then on, Klyde and I were business partners and friends.

Road Trip

Dear Lord,

Klyde and I joined forces with another team to win a trip to Chicago. We mapped out which cities we wanted to work. Klyde took every chance he got to flirt, but it didn't faze me because I had a boyfriend named Tommy. He lived near Mumford High School off 6 Mile and Wyoming. He was tall, about 6' 1", and had dreamy eyes. He had a laid back demeanor. He knew the right words to say to make my heart race. I got lost in his allure of sexy.

I talked about Tommy all the time to Klyde. He listened to me like a best friend would and he was the only person I confided in. I thought maybe, since he was a guy, he could give me some insight on how guys think.

I told Klyde about how Tommy didn't answer my calls most of the time. He almost never called me. I always went to his house to see him. Klyde advised me on how to handle him. He said if a person cared for me he'd answer my calls. The phone works both ways and I should not have to call him all the time. He told me the best way to get

Tommy's attention was to stop calling him. "If he misses you, he'll call you," he said. He also said to see how long it took for him to call and this would show me if he was really interested or not. "Then you will have your answer," he said.

I said okay. But, it was hard for me to stop calling him, so I didn't. Even Tommy's sister, Donita, told me to leave her brother alone. "Klyde brings you over here all the time," she said. "He seems like a good guy. You should talk to him and leave my brother alone. He's no good."

My brother Al let me drive his black Subaru to work and run errands. It was a stick shift. I wasn't a pro at driving it, but I made it where I needed to go. The day the Subaru broke down, I had no way to work. Since Klyde and I were friends and he was on my team, I asked him if he could pick me up and drop me off at work. "Not if you don't mind me flirting with you," he said. He was already flirting with me, so I said, "sure."

On the way to work, Klyde would ask me detailed personal questions like: do you have any kids, do you want any kids, do you plan to have any kids in the future, and do you have a savings and checking account. Once he even asked to see a picture of my mother to see what I would look like when I get older. He also told me he liked a woman with a big butt and thick thighs, an hourglass body. I didn't know why this was supposed to be important to me. First of all I didn't care and second, I had a boyfriend.

When I spoke to Klyde about Tommy, he said things like, "If you were mine, I'd never let you out of my sight. I would call you all the time." But it went in one ear and out the other. It didn't even make me blush. I would say thank you and keep it moving. I needed a ride, so I had to put up with his flirting.

I didn't have a car to drive to Tommy's house anymore, so Klyde dropped me off even though he thought I should leave Tommy alone and talk to him. "You're too beautiful to be ignored," he said. "You should date someone like me."

Eventually, I decided to put Tommy to the test. I refused to call or go by his house. Two weeks passed with nothing. No call! Really! I meant little to Tommy.

Klyde had already started moving in. We went out to eat at McDonald's. I paid half because I didn't want him to think we were on a date, plus I had my own money. I was independent and would never depend on a man. After two weeks, I started thinking about the things Klyde said to me. I paid more attention to him. He was different. I asked myself, who tries to help someone stay with her boyfriend. He must like me, right?

I became attracted to the way he thought. His mind, goals, and desires were all very alluring. He appeared confident. I liked a person with hopes and dreams who could make me laugh. But most of all, I liked a man who could have a good conversation.

After I decided to leave Tommy for good, guess who called, Tommy. My younger sister Soni answered the phone. I so happened to be standing right next to her when the call came in. I said, "Don't talk to him! Hang up! He's too late!" I told her to tell him I didn't want to talk to him. He said, "That's okay, I'll talk to you instead." I told her she better not talk to him and to hang up the phone and she did.

I realized he was not the right person for me. My mom taught me dating was learning about a person and determining if they are marriage material. Since I entered the dating scene, I've been looking for qualities I wanted in a husband. Maybe I should date a "preppy" guy; a guy trouble does not follow. I was not attracted to Klyde as a boyfriend, but I saw him every day and we had good conversations. He was the opposite of what I prayed for and wanted in my life.

Since Tommy was no longer a subject of discussion, I noticed more and more, how hard Klyde had been pushing and flirting. He shared his desire to move out of Michigan and into a warmer climate. He wanted to get away from the black cloud hovering over Detroit.

We both shared the desire to help the less fortunate and those who needed a little push. There were programs in place to help the poor, but not the ones who needed a little help. I found myself drawn to him.

We started to spend more and more time together. He would come over and pick me up and we'd sit in the car and talk. After my brother got his car fixed, I visited Klyde's parent's house. He came from a large family. His mother was five-feet tall with a nice shape, shoulder length hair, and calves built like a stallion. She was absolutely beautiful. Klyde's father, Klyde Sr., was 6' 2" and 250 pounds with an Afro. He talked even less than my dad.

We strolled down Clarita Street, up Curtis, and around the corner to Biltmore. He asked me a lot of questions: what did I like about him when I first saw him, had I ever been in a fight, had I ever been in love, what kind of alcohol did I drink.

I told him, I didn't like him at first. He looked

like a thug, but seemed interesting. I told him about one fight in elementary when a girl jumped on me because she thought I liked her boyfriend. She grabbed my hair, pulled it, and I socked her in the nose. I also told him I'd been in love and engaged to a man in Maryland, and I'd tried Colt 45 beer and I heard a drink called Cisco was good.

He told me stories about how he grew up. As a teenager, he got into a lot of trouble. He stole cars and went for joy rides and got stopped by the police. He was in and out of juvenile detention. Trouble followed him.

Walking home from school during his freshman year at Cooley High School, a boy followed him home. The boy ran up from behind, grabbed his neck, and demanded his shoes. Klyde said, "NO!" He pulled away and they got into a scuffle. Klyde picked up a brick and beat the boy in the head. He lost control and the boy died. The police took him to jail. He went to court and the judge ruled out first-degree murder and put him on probation because it was self-defense.

He said, "He didn't want me to hear it from someone else," but he thought I should know. He had to like me, right? Who would tell someone such a terrifying story unless he really liked them?

He didn't mean to kill anyone. After the courts

released him, his parents sent him south to Baton Rouge, Louisiana to live with his grandmother so he could stay out of trouble.

Ironically, down south he got into even more trouble. He stole cars and taught others how to steal them too. He ended up in a boys home for juvenile delinquents. Inside, he learned how to make a shank out of a toothbrush.

Years later, he still held the folk like he did in the penitentiary. He told me it was in case he had to stab somebody.

My mother taught me not to judge anyone. I believe anyone could change with God's help.

Liquid Crack

Dear Lord,

The following night Klyde picked me up to go to the drive-in movie theatre off Wyoming in Dearborn. He was a bit paranoid at times. We drove by Coney Island on 6 Mile and Wyoming when he picked up speed and suddenly started darting through traffic and dipping down side streets.

In his past, he sold drugs and roughed people up for Bob and Marley. I asked him if there were people looking for him. "You never can be too careful," he said. He went on to say he'd made a lot of money from selling drugs, over $17,000, but he got into a car accident and a lady sued him for $17,000. We dodged them and went to the movies. I never saw anyone.

I always did my best to do what was right. I tried. When we got to the drive-in, Klyde said, "I got something for you," and handed me a bottle of Strawberry Cisco. "You wanted to try this, didn't you," he said. I thought back on our previous conversations. I did mention I heard Cisco was good. It had a long, slender neck, sort of like a wine cooler and smelled like Kool-Aid.

I took a sip. It had a sweet, fruity, syrupy taste. I felt like I was drinking liquid love at first. Felt like the bottle was seducing me. I found myself sipping on Cisco, eating popcorn and watching less and less of the movie.

Then something happened. I didn't mean to move the cassette tape separating us. I didn't mean to hop onto his lap and do what I did. That wasn't me. But I enjoyed the long wet kiss. I enjoyed his hand caressing my face. I enjoyed a whole lot of things, until I didn't.

I was intoxicated, almost in a comatose state. What was I thinking? I wanted Klyde to like me. I remember him asking what I wanted to do and saying call your mother and let her know you are spending the night at a friend's house. "You know, you shouldn't go home drunk," he said. That's the last thing I remember.

I didn't remember the movie going off. I didn't remember the drive to the motel. I didn't remember getting out of the car and walking into the motel room, but what I do remember was waking up disorientated with a piercing stabbing pain.

I cried out, "Ouch! It hurts. Please stop!" When I looked into my lap blood was dripping between my legs and onto the sheets and along the side of the mattress. Inside I was burning. I crawled out from under him and turned over. The room was fairly small. I could see the door to the outside.

I sat up on the edge of a full sized bed. Across from the foot of the bed was a dresser; a nightstand on both sides of the bed. I reached for the nightstand. I tried to stand up, but I was on fire. My knees buckled. I grabbed my waist and staggered to the bathroom. Blood dripped while I saw him from the bathroom, sleeping, smiling in his sleep like a baby.

How did I allow this to happen? I didn't think he tried to hurt me, but he did. I spent the rest of the night in the bathroom on the toilet praying, crying, and trying not to scream. I was ashamed and disappointed in myself.

I was no longer proud of the flesh of my loins. My innocence had been silenced. After I came out of the bathroom, I stood by the side of the bed and looked at him. I shook his shoulder and told him I needed to go home NOW. No other words were exchanged. I was hurting. How would he have known how I really felt if I didn't tell him?

My Parent's Disappointment

Dear Lord,

How can I face my family? My family and I were close, loving, and compassionate. We looked out for each other. We always embraced one another with a hug. They looked at me and saw a quiet, shy, and naïve girl. They treated me like I was the baby sister and needed to be protected. My mom had always been supportive of me. She trusted me. I let her down. How could I act normal knowing what I'd been through? It was hard to breathe. I was traumatized. How was I supposed to process the sudden change in me? I felt like I was living a lie.

I walked into my parent's house with my head hung low. I was embarrassed and ashamed. I felt self-conscious. The heaviness was unbearable.

My mom asked if I was okay. "You don't seem yourself," she said. I assured her everything was fine. How could I tell her what I got myself into? I was keeping up a facade like everything was normal. The feeling of shame, guilt, and disappointment made me want to run and hide. She knew me too well. I was too scared. I waited as long as I could before I told her.

My mother asked when they were going to meet Klyde. "I see him come over, honk the horn, and you run out," she says. "This is not the way a man should treat a woman and this is not how you should allow yourself to be treated. Have respect for yourself, I taught you better." All I could say was yes, Mom. I gathered my things and left the house.

I didn't like disappointing my mom and dad. My dad taught me how to take care of myself, without a man. He was hard on men. He felt men should have a regular job and act as an entrepreneur on the side. The woman could work, but didn't have to. He felt women should be independent enough to handle things if their husbands passed away.

One weekend, my dad took me to his second job as a painter. I learned at a young age how to sand drywall, caulk, prim, trim, and paint. He wanted me to have skills no one could take away.

I wanted my dad to be proud of me. I wanted to have real estate property, to renovate, rent, and sell. But I wondered if my dream would come true after what happened.

When I got to my dad's house (my parents were separated) he had come from Eastern Market. Produce was all scattered along the kitchen table.

I could look at that, but I couldn't look at him. I helped my dad put away the groceries holding my head low because of my massive headache from a hangover. My dad was a man of few words, so when he spoke, you listened. He told me, "don't try to act like nothing's wrong with you." He had a certain look and I knew he saw right through me.

It didn't help any when my second oldest brother Edd told my dad I was going through something with Klyde. No one liked Klyde. They thought he was a good for nothing bum, but I couldn't see what they were talking about. I couldn't admit they might be right. I had to change this situation somehow. It was my fault this happened anyway.

Birth Control

Dear Lord,

I was eighteen and 105 lbs. I didn't know how to interact with Klyde after that night. I never experienced anything like it before. He thought nothing of it. It was like nothing happened.

I told my girlfriend I got drunk and how after drinking Cisco, I had a massive hangover for two days. She told me Cisco was dangerous, it was twenty percent alcohol forty proof. They called it "liquid crack." "You can die from alcohol poisoning," she said. She showed me an article from Time Magazine on the Internet.

After hearing this news, I was furious. I wanted to know if Klyde knew what he had given me. When I asked him if he knew what they called Cisco he gave me a strange look.

When I told him they called it liquid crack he laughed. People die from it! I told him about the written article. Then he stopped laughing and looked at me so cold, I felt a chill go up and down my spine. "You asked for it," he told me.

What did I know about alcohol, I was only eighteen! But he didn't put it to my mouth and make me drink either. So, I was partly at fault, right?

Klyde told me he was sorry. He said if he'd known it was dangerous, he would not have given it to me. I was glad to know he didn't mean to hurt me. He seemed sincere so I was over what happened. I put it behind me and moved on.

He still picked me up and dropped me off at work and home. He flirted all the time.

Klyde told me his friends thought I was too good for him. He told me he wanted us to be together forever.

Being one of eight children, I felt like an outcast. Not because my family made me feel that way, but because I was extremely quiet while everyone else was extremely outgoing. I felt invisible like an ugly duckling. Maybe I was adopted.

At times I would do things to get attention. Any attention was better than no attention. So when Klyde told me he wanted to be with me forever, I was happy. I told him the only thing I needed from him was love. Love me unconditionally. I didn't need a big house or fancy car. Only love. "Yes, I can do that," Klyde said.

We began seeing each other more and more. It had only been a couple of months, but I felt like we'd known each other for years. We talked about our future together: things we liked to do, marriage, having children years from now, places in other states we wanted to live. I thought, surely, this guy must really like me.

While we were discussing our future, Klyde showed me a calendar with names of woman next to the date he had sex with them. It was a bit scattered, about ten different people throughout the year, sometimes two people in a week. So I should trust him, right? He didn't have to show this to me. He stressed he did not want any kids right now. To make sure of it, he took me to Planned Parenthood to get birth control pills.

Getting pregnant was not an option. He told me he had too many goals and dreams to reach and having children would slow him down. I didn't like taking pills. I'd only taken aspirin a couple of times by throwing my head backward and taking a big gulp of water.

Pills were too hard for me to swallow. How was I going to take birth control pills every day? The doctor prescribed Ortho Tri-Cyclen, a pea sized pill, but I was not consistent with taking them. I wondered if it was a problem. Sex was no big deal to me. It didn't feel all that great, but it made Klyde happy. If I stopped having sex with him, I wondered if he'd still like me.

Doctor Call

Dear Lord,

I would never forget the day of the doctor's visit. I sat on the examination table with my legs dangling, waiting. He said he'd be back with test results. As I waited thoughts raced through my mind. How did this happen? I was on birth control, but I had not been taking them every day. Could this be the cause? I didn't think about the consequences of having sex.

When the doctor came back he had a happy and sad face. It was like he couldn't decide which one fit what he was about to say. He said, "You're pregnant," and a tremor went through my body. I couldn't breathe. A million things ran through my head, but nothing came out of my mouth. It was complete and utter paralyzing panic.

My first instinct was to run and hide somewhere no one would ever find me. So I hid from myself. I didn't want to look in the mirror. I didn't like who was looking back. That girl was pregnant; a statistic; a disappointment to herself and her family. I made a mistake and I didn't know how to fix it. I didn't know how to tell my mother, father, siblings, and boyfriend.

So, I told Klyde first, and he asked me if it was his. Wow! How could he say that? "What are you going to do," he asked. "Do you want to keep it? I'll pay for an abortion. It's whatever you want to do, I'm okay with it."

In my mind, there was never a question. I really wasn't giving him a say in the matter. I was firm with my response. "I'm keeping my baby," I said, regardless if he was in the baby's life or not. It's crazy, but there was no way in this world I was having an abortion, mainly because it was against my religion. But so was fornication.

Lord, how could I disappoint you so badly; I never wanted to have a child out of wedlock. I didn't want to be a hypocrite, nor a statistic. Nineteen and pregnant, I was like every other teenager mother. I had sex before marriage and everyone knew it.

Would I be able to nurture and provide the proper care a child needed? What type of relationship would we have as mother and child? What would the effects be on the child as a result of me being an unwed mother?

What would people say to me? How could I teach him or her not to have sex before marriage and don't get pregnant at a young age? What could I really tell my baby now?

Busted

Dear Lord,

I sat at the dining room table with my family. Everyone was happy. Everyone was what they always had been, except me.

I pushed away from the table, jumped up, and ran to the bathroom. I was on my knees with the toilet rim inches from my face. When I was done, I wanted to stay there. I didn't want to leave.

My mother came in, looking intensely into my soul, shaking her head. "You're pregnant, aren't you," she said. After about a minute, I told her yes. I saw the disappointment in her face. No excitement, only disappointment. I was disappointed too.

My mother always said, "Don't grow up too fast, stay young as long as you can." Nevertheless, there I was. No turning back. My childhood was over.

I was forced to grow up. But I didn't want to. I didn't know how. I saw what was going on, but didn't want to admit it. I didn't want to say anything out loud.

Lamentations 1:20

See, o Lord, that I am in distress;
My soul is troubled; My heart is
overturned within me,
For I have been rebellious.
Will I ever be able to forgive myself?

Chapter 3
EXPOSED

Dear Lord,

My mother stood over the kitchen sink overlooking the dining room, shucking ears of corn. All of a sudden she said, "You are going to have a bastard child." Out of the blue, she never stopped picking at the corn.

How was I supposed to react? What was I supposed to do? I didn't believe in talking back to my parents. So I said nothing. Even though it was painful to hear those words, I knew she loved me.

I didn't quite understand what bastard meant so I went to Webster's dictionary and found out it meant a child born out of wedlock. But it sounded so harsh.

After helping my mother in the kitchen, I went by my dad's house for dinner. He made candied yams, collard greens, fried corn, and red beans and rice.

Without notice, my father looked straight ahead with a mouth full of red beans and rice said, "You got to have an abortion. He can't take care of you. He doesn't have a job. Walking door to door trying to sell bottled perfume is not a job. Your brother is going to take you, don't worry."

My dad was a laid back man of few words, so I knew he meant every word. I said, "But, Dad!" I changed my mind mid-sentence and looked down. I finished eating, cleaned the kitchen, and went home.

I couldn't kill a child. I already committed one sin by having sex out of wedlock. I wanted to do what was right. But the pregnancy sparked other problems.

While standing in the kitchen at Klyde's mother's (Beatrice) house she walked up to me and whispered in my ear, "Please don't leave Klyde. He can't take getting hurt again." Beatrice told us if we didn't get married it would be an abomination against God. Klyde would not be allowed back in church. I didn't want to be the cause of God leaving Klyde's life. I disobeyed God once; I didn't want to do it again.

So what could I do to fix this? All I could think

about was Romans 6:23: "For the wages of sin is death, but the gift of God is eternal life in [a] Christ Jesus our Lord." I sinned by having sex before marriage. Klyde's salvation was important to me and I wanted God to forgive me.

We both agreed we didn't want anyone to pressure us into getting married. But I didn't want to be a single mother either. I asked the Lord for forgiveness and mercy.

True Colors

Dear Lord,

Pregnant and working at Creative Concepts was not the future I envisioned for myself. So I got a job at Kerby's Koney Island in Northland Mall as a waitress. I needed to save money before the baby was born.

My cousins, Angelica and Tonya, also worked there. The job only paid $2.25 per hour, but the rest was supposed to be made up in tips. I hoped so. I was starting to feel like a burden on my mother. I was pregnant, and I didn't like the way Klyde treated me. He pushed me off on my mother.

Once, I told Klyde I was hungry and he slammed on the brakes and did a 360-degree turn. I thought he was taking me to get something to eat, but instead, pulled in front of my mother's house, and dropped me off at the curb.

Once we started dating, I knew Klyde would meet my mom. He said he didn't want to meet the family until he knew for sure we were going to be together. I told him it was disrespectful to blow the horn for me to come out. He should walk to the door and ring the bell and when taking me home, he should walk me to the door. Like a real gentleman would.

I was running out of excuses. My mom peeked out the living room curtains. That was my signal it was time to come inside. I said my goodbyes and went into the house. I saw what was going on but didn't want to speak it into existence.

Klyde, Met Mom

Dear Lord,

Klyde finally met my mom. Immediately he went to comparing us. "You both have high cheekbones, the same smile and eyes," he said. " Oh, you're beautiful. I see where your daughter gets her looks." He even said, "Before you get into a relationship with a female, you have to look at the mother in order to see how the daughter is going to turn out. If the momma's small, the daughter most likely will be to. If the mother is fat, her daughter will be fat too. I don't want anything big, but a house, car, and bank account."

My mother looked at him in a way only a mother can. Her brows were raised and she squinted a bit in disbelief. She said, "It takes more than looks to maintain a relationship. As we grow older, our physical appearances change. No one remains the same." Then she walked away.

My mom pulled me aside and said, "There's something not right about him." She said he was putting too much emphasis on looks and made her feel uncomfortable. "I can see problems in the future. I'm concerned his priorities and morals are not in line with the word of God. It's something about him I can't put my finger on, but be careful," she said.

I wanted to listen to her but I liked him. It seemed like he had a good heart, but a little different mind. I prayed, Lord, let your light shine within him.

Ex's vs. Me

Dear Lord,

Pregnant with Klyde's baby, I felt it was rude and disrespectful to allow his ex-girlfriend to come by his mother's house. At first it didn't bother me, but actually, several women would come by her house. Taron and Nichola visited most often. Taron was the girl he fell in love with before he met me and broke his heart. She had a daughter by another man. Klyde found out after dating for a year that she was still sleeping with her baby's daddy. They planned to move into an apartment together before we met. He even showed me the apartment.

I asked Beatrice why she let Klyde's ex-girlfriends come over, especially considering I was pregnant with his baby. "Baby, you aren't married to my son and he has no ties to you. No offense, honey," she said. What I heard Beatrice say was I really didn't matter. I felt a swift kick in my chest that comment. I told Klyde what she said. He told me he couldn't control what his mother did in her house.

After seeing Klyde's ex-girlfriends interact with

his mother, I saw why the girls kept coming over. She was sweet, kind, and funny. I told Klyde I understood. No worries, I was going to start visiting my ex-boyfriend's mother. She was sweet, kind, and caring too. She was a foster mother who adopted several children. She treated them as if they were her own. They were like my little brothers and sisters. I miss them all.

I went to Ms. Carol's house and knocked on the door. She greeted me with a warm and inviting smile. She hugged me and kissed my check. We sat in the living room talking and sharing stories. I learned to appreciate the importance of relationships. Once you find kindhearted people, you hang onto them no matter what.

After I told Klyde I visited my ex-boyfriend's mother, I didn't see any more women visiting his mother. But it wasn't that simple. Nichola, who lived in Ohio, wouldn't let Klyde go. She had to stay connected. She asked Beatrice to be her daughter's Godmother. How convenient. Beatrice told Klyde she didn't see anything wrong with it. And that was the end of that.

Later on, Klyde told me his sisters, Debra and Charlene, arranged for Nichola to come to Michigan and take him away from me. They thought I was homely and too shy. I was not a good match for him. It didn't matter I was pregnant with their brother's baby. I didn't know they felt this way about me. But it didn't change the way I felt around them. It was not in me to hold grudges or mistreat anyone. My greatest fear was being a statistic and left alone to raise the baby. I knew things were going to get better.

Pass or Fail

Dear Lord,

I felt staying at my dad's apartment was best. My dad had no problem with me moving in, but "that Ninja can't stay here," he said. My dad didn't know Klyde and wanted to find out what was on his mind and talk to him about his responsibilities. I told Klyde my dad wanted to talk to him about taking care of the baby and me.

When Klyde knocked on the door I stood on my tippy toes and looked through the peephole before I opened it. My dad, standing off to the side, told me to open the door. He looked hard and stern. Klyde said hello and asked if he could take a seat on the sofa next to me.

My dad immediately said, "I want to talk to you about my daughter. Are you a man? Do you know what a man's responsibilities are? You are equally responsible for her getting pregnant. You have to take care of the baby and make sure my daughter is taken care of. During the pregnancy you should make sure she's eating and has a peace of mind."

I listened as Klyde told my dad the only person he was responsible for was the baby I was carrying. My heart skipped a beat, then stopped, dropped, and rolled. I scooted away, slightly in disbelief. At the same time, I was trying not to show my true feelings to my dad. I could not believe what I was hearing. My head dropped. I was so let down. The man I was having a baby with didn't want to look after my well-being.

I felt used and wondered if the relationship would last. So, it was as my daddy told me. He was going to leave me barefoot and pregnant. OK, legally that may be the case; he didn't have to take care of me. But he shouldn't have told his girlfriend's father that, especially not with her sitting right there.

My dad wanted to hurt him. I could see it. He flat told him, "GET OUT! You're a no good for nothing ninja." But he used the other N word. "You don't even have a pot to piss in. You're no man. Get out! And don't come back," he said.

My dad thought Klyde was ignorant and an irresponsible boy. He felt if you get a woman pregnant, you should step up and take care of not only the baby, but her too. Klyde said, "No disrespect, but my only responsibility is to the baby." He then looked at me and said goodbye.

Did he really believe this, I wondered. If I could change him mind. He told me he loved me. "I want to feel every bit of you, your mind and body," he said. The love Klyde said he had for me must not be real. But in my heart, I felt he loved me.

Klyde's dad put him out on his 21st birthday so he could become a man. But he didn't have a place to lay his head at night. So he slept in his car. I still felt attached to Klyde, even after he told my dad he had no attachment to me. Why was I so hardheaded, stubborn, and strong-minded? I didn't listen to wise counsel.

Six months pregnant and sleeping on my dad's sofa bed in the living room. Yet, I felt sorry for Klyde sleeping in his car. He parked down the street at night. After my dad fell asleep, I would sneak out and sleep in the car with him. Being I was seven months pregnant, it was very uncomfortable. I felt sorry for him and wanted to be close to him. Before my dad woke up, I'd quietly sneak back in.

My life was a struggle because I was pregnant, single with no money. My family shunned me. They were hurt and disappointed. I was hurt and disappointed in myself.

Chapter 4

Pregnant with a Sexually Transmitted Disease

Dear Lord,

Ｗhile working at Kerby's Koney Island, my stomach and back started cramping. It was insanely intense. I felt like I had a boulder sitting on top of me. As the day continued, I noticed my walk even started to change. I was like a penguin holding baby eggs between his legs. I asked my cousins Angelica and Tonya to take me to the hospital.

At the hospital, a male gynecologist examined me. I was nervous because it was a man. What could he tell me about my body, he's a man! I got on the examination table. My vagina felt like someone had put their foot inside of me. So the doctor took samples.

When he came back, he told me to drink a lot of water and get some rest.

I went home and followed the doctor's orders. I drank lots of water rested. I woke up the following morning with a big soft bubble between my legs. I couldn't close them. This time, I went to Providence Hospital's Emergency Room. As I lay on the examination table, the big mass between my legs kept growing. The doctor ran tests and came back with results; I had three sexually transmitted diseases.

I was eight months pregnant, with three sexually transmitted diseases! How could this be? The only person I had sex with was Klyde. I remembered last year he showed me a calendar with women he had sex with before me. He told me I was the only one since he'd been with me. So how could that be?

I was scared and upset, so I confronted him. He said he didn't have any symptoms and he'd only been with me. If he *did* have anything, he said, it's because *I* gave it to *him*. After he allegedly went to the doctor, he said the test results came back negative for any (STDs) sexually transmitted diseases.

I asked him to show me proof. He said they

didn't give him anything because he didn't have anything. If he did they would have, he told me. Then he started accusing me. I was not having sex with anyone else. Klyde told me people have things in their bodies but are dormant and maybe that's what was happening. So I let it go.

I couldn't possibly tell my family. They would say, "I told you so." I could barely sit. I was bedridden. I tried to walk, but I couldn't. Klyde asked his mother Beatrice if I could stay with her. Her sofa let out into a king sized bed. She had a babysitting business in the basement where I slept. I felt swollen like a sumo wrestler. I couldn't move until the infection burst. How embarrassing. Beatrice fixed me food and took care of me.

Was this a warning sign? A sign of betrayal telling me how our relationship was going to be? Or should I've believed him when he told me it was some freak accident. I asked the Lord to give me a sign so I'd know the truth.

Bundle of Joy

Dear Lord,

The labor pains hurt so badly. The contractions were ten minutes apart when I called Klyde to have him pick me up from my dad's house. He took me to Providence hospital. I was under my dad's insurance, but I recently signed up for Medicaid. I told the hospital I had Blue Cross and Blue Shield, but they said Medicaid was primary. They put me in a room with five other pregnant women. I knew this wasn't right. I told Klyde and the nurses I was supposed to be in a semi private room. It didn't matter. The pain worsened.

They asked me if I wanted an epidural. I said no. I didn't want any drugs to transfer to my baby. At the last minute, I asked if I could have something, but it was too late. The pressure was so severe. It felt like a bowel movement, but it was the baby's head knocking at my door. It was time to push. I gave one big push. Oh, it felt good. "Can I push again," I said. They said no, I needed to wait a minute.

Ok... push.... Yes.... Push again.... Yes... it's a girl!

December 18, 1989, two weeks before my due date, but exactly on the destined date, my daughter was born. It was 6 a.m. on an arctic day, a record low, minus three degrees. Like millions of other mothers, my baby caressed my heart with passion. I held her in the warmth of my arms as she gazed up at me with her russet eyes, vulnerably fluttering.

She had long dark chocolate wavy hair and her delicate fingers occasionally unlocked and locked as she shattered the silence with screeching. I was surprised it was a girl. I only had boy's names picked out. Raphael Armani. But not for a girl. I thought about Gabriel Armani, but Klyde said people would call her Gabby and gabby meant she talked a lot. I didn't want that, but I thought this was a nice way of Klyde saying he didn't like the name and it worked.

Klyde and his friend from Baton Rouge came to see me at the hospital after I had the baby. He had a list of baby names. One was an ex-girlfriend's sister's name, Jade. I knew what the name meant and liked it. I liked the name so much I decided to use it.

Relieved that the delivery went well, Klyde came to the hospital with a rental agreement that his friend, Pastor J. Everso, a real estate broker, had drawn up. He said he found a two bedroom, one bathroom bungalow off Plymouth and Montrose and if we could come up with $770, we could move in. The rent would be $335 a month. I gave him the money and we were able to move in when I left the hospital.

This was the only place we could afford on my income, since Klyde wasn't working. Outside of the house, I felt no safety; the neighborhood was foreign to me. As I sat, I heard the shrill, high-pitched sound of sirens. The police raced down the street. I ducked. I never knew if my window was going to be shattered by a stray bullet. I suppose I was a bit naive when it came to the real world. That's what my father told me.

Despite the fact, my mother raised me well. I was a young mother with no sense of how to take care of a baby. I was scared, completely terrified, and didn't know what to do.

Blocking out the background noise, I looked down at my baby girl. This came out of me. While lying in bed, in my new house with Klyde and Jade, the doorbell rang. This was the first time Klyde and I had our own space. I'd never seen a man naked before Klyde. When he got out of the bed, I peeked shyly out the side of my eye to fully look at him. He grabbed his clothes and put them on.   I was really grown-up now.

My mother Ruth and sister Soni came in the door with breakfast. They didn't come to the hospital to see Jade, so this was a perfect time. I heard my mom's voice. I called out to her, "I'm back here in my room." As they walked through the living room Klyde stopped them. "No, I'll bring the baby in here," he said. I didn't know what that was all about. I'd never seen him act that way. I had a baby and needed love and support. I needed my mother. I was scared to open my legs again.

My mother told me she didn't feel comfortable coming over, but she loved me. They left. I really needed my mother's help with the baby. With Jade needing to be fed in the middle of the night, I felt sleep-deprived. I was miserable and needed help.

I asked Klyde why did he stop my mom from coming into our bedroom to see the baby and me and he said they walked in like the owned the place. He did not want people walking through his house. I felt he was being territorial, how a dog marks and guards his turf.

Since he ran my family off I asked Klyde to fix me something to eat. He went into the kitchen to prepare lunch. I heard running water, pots, and pans. Two hours later, I was wondering what was taking so long. I needed to eat to be able to breast feed. I called out to Klyde. He said it wasn't ready yet. My stomach was growling. I started to think I was going to starve. I couldn't go on like this. I needed my mother.

The Shock of Abuse

Oh Lord, it had only been two weeks since I delivered my sweet baby girl. How could this have happened? How could I make him stop? I yelled, "STOP! STOP! PLEASE STOP!"

My voice became spineless and fragile until it was as if every breath I took was departing my lifeless body. My life became something unreal, like a vision of someone else's life. Not a vision I could ever imagine. Not a vision I would ever want to. The light went dim. He squeezed tighter and tighter and I started to suffocate.

I saw a bright light, the heavens. All I could say in my mind was Jesus! Jesus! Jesus! There was no doubt in my mind I was dying. Then I felt a release.

Lying there, lifeless and limp, I thought about my mother's words. "If a man hits you once, he'll hit you again," she said. But I didn't want to believe it, let alone tell my family Klyde is exactly the man they thought he was.

I didn't call the police. Klyde caressed my face and asked why I made him do it. "I'm sorry; I didn't mean to hurt you," he said.

While I sobbed and cried uncontrollably I told him he tried to kill me. He said it wasn't that bad. "I only squeezed with one hand a little, I wasn't trying to kill you." Klyde pulled me toward him and held me in his arms, rocking back and forth, saying he loved me. "It's okay," he said. "I'll never do it again. You're not going to leave me are you?"

My mother's words resonated in my mind. "He hit you once, he'll hit you again." I wanted to tell her, but I couldn't. It would prove her right. So I stayed silent, broken, and frightened. I didn't know what to do.

Klyde asked me whether I was leaving him. With a somber and fragile voice, I said no. What was I supposed to say? This man tried to kill me, and then tried to convince me he didn't. "It wasn't that bad," he said. He wiped off my face, warmed up my food, and then continued on as if nothing happened.

Lord, what did I do to deserve this? Help him with this rage and anger.

Who Am I

Dear Lord,

Since the baby was here, Klyde was on me about finding a job. He sat me down and said, "In order for us to move forward, you need to get a job." He said if I didn't, it would take us a long time to move out of this house.

So I talked to my friend Martha about finding a job. She worked at Farmington Hills Nursing Home. Martha said they were hiring and I should apply. I applied and got the job right away. A five-week training course taught me all I needed to know about taking care of senior citizens. I became a Certified Nursing Assistant (CNA) at Farmington Nursing Home in Farmington Hills.

I loved my job. I liked the wisdom all around me. However, having this job meant waking up at 4:00 a.m. to shower, dress, wake Jade up, wash her and give her a bottle. The routine made me feel like a robot. I did the same thing every day. By 5:15 every morning, I was out the door driving down Southfield Freeway to drop Jade off at her Grandma Beatrice's house. Then off to work.

I punched in the clock by 5:50 a.m. I tried to get in early so I could have time to eat breakfast, but Klyde insisted I call him first to let him know I made it to work. My first thought was he's trying to keep tabs on me. So I asked, why and he said he wanted to make sure I made it to work safely. Sound reasonable to me, even made me feel like he cared.

As a nursing assistant I bathed and shower men and woman like I did my child. The difference was instead of a 30 lb. baby, I was assigned a 300 lb. woman. I only weigh 90 lbs. I was the smallest one there so I didn't know why they would assign her to me. Her name was Cathy. She was a very sweet lady. Sometimes I gave her a bed bath and other times a shower. She had a stroke so the left side of her body was paralyzed. Whenever I gave her a shower I had to use a Hoyer lift and she was not the only patient I had. I typically had five.

After I showered them all I took them to breakfast. One of my patients was bed ridden. She had a colostomy bag attached to her stomach. She had to eat a brand cereal on a daily basis to ensure she defecated at least once a day.

Working at my home after working at the

nursing home was taking a toll on me. I loved taking care of older people, but catering to them all day, then coming home and doing the same thing with Klyde and Jade was stressful. The patients were continuously calling my name. I would go home tired and in need of a break. But of course all I heard was "Mommy, mommy, mommy!"

It was not fair for my daughter to suffer because I had to work. It was frustrating because I didn't realize I was going to be working, cooking, cleaning, and taking care of my daughter all by myself. I did everything. I knew this was not what God had planned for me.

I dreaded going home almost every day. Something was wrong with this picture. Life was miserable. I actually imagined getting into a car accident on some days. I'd do anything to keep from going home. I wanted the freedom to feel loved and give love to my little girl. Lord, help me.

My Faith or My Man

Dear Lord,

I was so confused I didn't know where my place in life was anymore. I was not living the life my mother raised me to live. I was taught family values and the importance of marriage. In order to have a purpose in our lives, we need to recognize the source of life. It was necessary for growth. I was separated from all I knew. I felt isolated from my family and the world. I felt like something was lost. I missed going to the Kingdom Hall and fellowshipping.

I didn't realize how much God meant to me. Since I didn't want to hold Klyde back from his church, I needed to learn more about the Pentecostal Apostolic Church.

Before I started going to Klyde's church, I requested a meeting with Pastor Wyndham. I told him before I could be a part of this church I had a few questions. I asked if he believed and taught the word of God in the bible; did he believe in the trinity; and what were the church doctrinal beliefs. However, my main question was if he believed God's name was Jehovah. He said yes and sealed the deal. I was pleased to hear this because I wanted to support my husband.

At this church, I still felt out of place and a bit scared. I wore miniskirts to church, and hairdos that stood out. I told the pastor I didn't have any other clothes to wear. He said, "come as you are and don't worry about anyone." If someone said anything to me, I should let him know. He became a person I could trust and talk to.

What scared me were the church members, the outburst of screaming, and speaking in tongues. Several people held the pews, rocked back and forward, jumping up and down and running around the church. They called it the Holy Ghost Dance. The pastor sounded like he was rapping and had something caught in his throat. This was so different from the Jehovah Witnesses.

At my old church, the Kingdom Hall, we sat quietly and listened to the minister teach. We sang a mellow song in unison. But not here! Excitement was all around. The energy was high, from the singing to the preaching. I enjoyed the music, but I enjoyed the preacher more. The word of God penetrated my heart and tears rolled down my face when I heard something relating to my life. I longed to hear the voice of the Lord again and I heard through the Pastor.

Scars and Bruises

Dear Lord,

Klyde beat me again, but this time I ran out of the house butt-naked. I got into the car and locked the doors. He banged on the door and said, "Open up, come back in the house." But I was too scared. He called his mother Beatrice. I'm not sure what he told her, but she came over, looked in the blue nova, and saw me curled up in the corner trying to cover my naked body. She pleaded with me to get out of the car and get some clothes on. Klyde wanted to talk to me and apologize she said.

I was embarrassed Beatrice had to witness this and see my naked body. She brought me a towel to cover up with. I got out of the car, but was scared to go in the house. Klyde handed me some clothes. I stood in the living room and put my underwear on, then the t-shirt. The next thing I knew, he was talking and riling himself up. Then he started hitting me and pushed me into the wall. I tried to run, but he grabbed me.

I screamed, but he clamped his hands over

my mouth and shoved me against the wall. Then he picked me up over his head and threw me across the room. I landed face first on the floor. He said, "You tried to run from me." Beatrice stood doing nothing, I guess in surprise and disbelief. She yelled for Klyde to stop and put me down. "You're going to hurt her," she said. But he didn't listen.

Sharp pains riveted my body, from my head to my feet. Blood dripped down my face. I wanted to grab my baby girl, but I was scared. I looked back at her while running to the door. I didn't know if I could make it out of the house. I prayed he wouldn't hurt our baby. I didn't know what was causing these attacks. I looked in the mirror at the scars left behind, some visual and some not. He was bleeding me dry of any love and affection I had for him. I didn't know where to go. I thought about the women's shelter.

I couldn't afford to take off work, so I had to go to the shelter. When I went to work everyone looked at me because my skin was missing from the center of my forehead down to the tip of my lip. I told everyone I was in a bad car accident. I went on as if things were normal, but after work Jade and I would go to the shelter. I was determined to find out what was wrong with me. What was I doing to make him so angry?

Was I crazy for trying to make the relationship work? I couldn't let my family know. I couldn't let them be right about him. I didn't want to be a single mother.

Psalms 27:1

The LORD is my light and my salvation;
whom shall I fear?
The LORD is the stronghold of my life
of whom shall I be afraid?

Chapter 5
Proceed with Caution

Dear Lord,

Klyde decided he wanted to get married. So I started to plan a June wedding, but Klyde said he didn't have time and changed it to February. I pleaded with him to wait until it was warmer outside. "If I don't get married, they're going to draft me," he said. I didn't want him to get drafted, so I told my family, and they rushed to plan a wedding. My dad didn't approve.

We had two weeks. My mother and brother Al baked the cakes and made the food. My brother Drew bought my wedding dress for me. I found a dress at Dave's bridal shop in Ferndale for $200. My dress was long and white with a removable train. Beautiful!

We were already living together so nothing would change really. A piece of paper would make it legal and bonding (official). Before we got our marriage license we went to the welfare office to tell them we were getting married. They were helping me with food stamps and health insurance. Klyde told them it was a shame we were going to get penalized for getting married because the state was going to stop helping, but that's the way it worked. If we were getting married, it was not the state's responsibility to take care of us. It fell on the man. Under these circumstances, there was no other option. Klyde had to get married to avoid the draft.

I really didn't know if getting married would solve our problems, but I was hoping it would. Klyde's friend Marley asked him if he was sure he was ready to get married. My older sister and sister-in-law wondered the same thing. Denise and my sister-in-law, Christine, came over before the wedding to ask if I was sure I was doing the right thing. They told me I had already made one mistake and I didn't need to make another. I took offense to what they said. It made me want to try even harder to make the marriage work.

My bridal shower was in my mother's basement. Even though they didn't agree with the marriage, they all supported my decision. It meant a lot.

Valentine's Day

Dear Lord,

My wedding day was an interesting day. Before the ceremony, we went out to a few businesses and plowed snow. Klyde cut grass in the summer and plowed snow in the winter. He also worked at a hair salon. Neither of which brought home much money.

Afterward, I rushed LaWanna to finish my hair because Klyde threatened not to marry me if I was late. He didn't want to look bad standing at the altar by himself. I was scared; he meant it... I wanted to be married to the father of my child. I was hurt and disappointed. I didn't understand why he would say that if he loved me.

We married in Pastor Wyndham's office on Thursday, February 14, 1991. My dad refused to come. He went to work instead. My sister stood in as my maid of honor and my brother gave me away. My wedding day was not very magical. I had sex before marriage and we were already living together. It was stressful and I was nervous. My family kept looking at me. I kept debating going through with it.

I laughed during the entire ceremony. A lot of things were going on in my mind. He actually told me the wedding was off if I didn't make it on time. He beat me and was verbally abusive. We didn't have money and my family didn't know he bought my wedding ring from a crack head.

We waited until the next day to have the wedding reception. I drank so much I got drunk. My friend Angel helped me to the bathroom. She helped me out of the big white dress and into a two piece cream and gold suit my sisters bought me as a wedding gift. I walked back to the reception, but not for long. I was so drunk I couldn't walk without stumbling. Klyde carried me to the Jeep and we went home.

The following day, we were supposed to go on our honeymoon, but I woke up to a snow blizzard. We decided to go anyway to celebrate our union. We headed north. The further we got the heavier the snow, until the road and sky were completely white.

We couldn't see the lines on the highway, let alone a car in front of us. We were driving ten miles per hour, if that. The snow was worse than the northwest side of Detroit. When we got to the hotel, it was a ratchet awful mess.

The hotel was nothing like the brochure. We went back home through a snowstorm and spent the rest of the day watching TV.

Alcohol is My Best Friend

Dear Lord,

The strain of lifting people twice my size had taken its toll on me so I started a new job at Mercy Health Services as a file clerk. My office hours were 6 a.m. to 2:30 p.m. I dropped Jade off at Klyde's mother's house at 5:30 a.m. I didn't feel right leaving a man at home in bed while I went to work.

Klyde had a "white complex." All he talked about was how the white man was keeping him down. He was so paranoid. When I got the job in white collar America he started accusing me of running off with a white man. Was he paranoid or was he concerned? I called him from the payphone when I got to work and when I was on the way home. I always heard if accused then guilty.

I couldn't take the mental torture anymore. I had good insurance through my job. I started seeing a psychologist on my lunch break. I kept it a secret from Klyde. I needed someone to talk to. My daddy always told me to watch and see. "He's going to leave you barefoot and pregnant," he said. "You can do bad by yourself, you don't need a man."

He said things like this because he didn't like seeing me struggle. My dad taught me to be an independent woman, to never depend on a man. But I wanted to be a supportive wife to my husband, not one who wreaked havoc on her home. I wanted to keep the peace. I searched the scriptures for advice on how to be a submissive wife.

I didn't want him to believe I was holding back, but I was gradually being stripped of my identity. I depended more and more on Klyde. I'd been mesmerized by his dreams and desires. I didn't think for myself. He told me it was better this way, he was protecting me from making mistakes.

He was so convincing I second-guessed myself. Instead of defending myself I sat back and listened with a puzzled look. Sometimes I felt like I was losing my mind. I thought about how I could make the pain go away. As I drove down side streets I prepared myself to get hit by oncoming traffic.

I felt less than a person around Klyde. He threatened me. If I left him no one would want me and my baby, he said. After work I had to stay home, take care of the house, and make sure he had something to eat when he came home. He came and went as often as he pleased. I never knew the places he went.

If I wanted to run to CVS, I had to ask him to babysit his own child. Most of the time the answer was no, but if he happened to say yes I had to come right back.

Klyde didn't like me being around my family or friends since we were a couple. He said I was supposed to separate from my family and friends and cleave toward him so we can become one. I wanted to be obedient to God's words, but I didn't think this was right.

Since I couldn't go around those I loved, I wanted him around all the time. I felt isolated from the outside world. When he was gone, I wanted him home. Once, I called his pager six times: 7 p.m., 7:05, 7:15, 7:30, 7:45, and 8:00. It had been two months since our wedding. No answers, no returned calls. I worried day in and day out. Where was he?

When he finally came home, I was excited, not mad. I didn't want to be a nagging wife. I found myself wondering what was wrong with me.

His behavior changed, he acted strange. His sex drive was usually extraordinarily high. It was sex before breakfast and before *and* after I fell asleep. But now he was not jumping on top of me as soon as I hit the sheets. Something was off.

I asked him what was wrong. With a somber look he turned away and said, he made a mistake. "I had sex...with one of my clients," he said. I wanted to know when, why, where, and every detail. He said he stayed late one night at work, doing a client's hair, and she approached him strongly.

They went out to the car, but he didn't cum. He got caught up in the "moment." He felt vulnerable and she said all the right things to made him feel good and wanted. Then he turned it on me. He said, I needed to compliment him like other women. I needed to show I wanted him. I didn't believe in lying so I couldn't give him this.

Why did we get married? I felt like calling it quits. But that was the easy way. I stood by biblical principles and was going to work on my marriage. So to show him how much he meant to me, I pleased him over and over all day: Before the break of dawn, when he woke up in the morning, midday, evening, and in the midnight hours. I wanted to please my husband. If I pleased him, he wouldn't go astray again, right?

After the affair I became numb. I drank

alcohol to tolerate sex with him. I didn't want to feel any pleasure from him. When Klyde climbed on top of me, I told my mind it didn't feel good. I laid there lifeless. I cried and hurt with disappointment. Tears rolled down the side of my face.

21 Years Old, Married with Child

Dear Lord,

Klyde threw me a surprise birthday party at the Marriott. I should have been happy. He drove up to the hotel and said he wanted to take a look at one of the suites. He asked me to come in with him. I didn't care to go in, but I went anyway. He went to the front counter and said he wanted to view one of their rooms. The front desk gave him a room key and we headed up to the 3rd floor. He told me to open the door. I opened the door, the light flickered on, and everyone yelled, "Surprise!"

Oh, surprise for sure. I took a deep breath as I entered the room, I looked around quickly, said thank you, and went into the bedroom. Everyone invited were his friends. I sat and reflected on my life. I was twenty one years old, married with a baby, abused and mistreated. I never envisioned this life.

I was so sad. I couldn't stop crying. I didn't talk a lot, so I didn't know what to say when I went back out. Klyde came in and gave me a drink. It was what I needed to loosen up. I got another and listened to his friends' conversations. I smiled and listened. I was not having fun. Was this really what I chose for my life?

I couldn't stand Klyde. In order to deal with the mental and physical abuse and the unhappiness at home, I turned to alcohol. At first, I would drink enough to get a buzz. It put me in a state of mind that numbed my feelings. Then, I was able to perform my wifely duties without showing resentment. I felt like a slave, a trophy. He showed me off like an object on display to his friends but treated me like a sex toy and beat me behind closed doors. But what was I to me?

Did I make the wrong choice for a husband? Was I being punished for disobeying God? I wanted to desire him, but I despised him. He was not the kind of husband I needed. He was a cheater and a wife beater. I put on the public face. To the world I was happy, like the queen of England. I thought of myself as the first lady. I couldn't let the church, or my family, see the relationship for what it really was. It would tarnish the congregation. If I failed, so would others.

Peaceful times never lasted long in our house. I sat in my room reading a book when Klyde tried to hurt my feelings. In a monotone voice, he told me he loved God more than me. "He is my first love, not you," he said.

Truthfully, for me to hear I was not his first love stung a little. But God should be the head of life, so I let it roll off. But he kept beating me down with words and making me feel stupid. He said things like, "That's why you're bald headed and skinny." It didn't work. I told him, "I cut my hair! I didn't have any problems growing hair." Then he said, "Your butt look nasty in those jeans, especially the ones with no pockets on the back. You never did look good in jeans. You should never wear them again."

It began to escalate. He said I was irresponsible; I'd leave the door unlocked, and lose the house keys inside the house. "You're nothing without me," he said. "The women I used to talk to all had money, their hair was always done, and they wore nice clothes." He said he liked women who are thick, with nice thighs, and a big booty. He didn't consider these attributes as out of shape but an hourglass body. He told me if I got fat, he'd leave.

I was neither thick nor had a big booty, and not a fat gene in my body. He paced the floor twitching and saying he missed fighting. He cracked his knuckles and neck like kernels of popcorn. He accused me of being nonchalant. I didn't care about not having money to pay bills. I told him idle words didn't hurt me. It took two to argue and I was not going to be one of them. Instead, I looked at him and said, "I love you!"

He said I was looking at him the way his dad looks at his mother. Then he went from Dr. Jekyll to Mr. Hyde. It was like he was possessed by a demon. His face exploded. I thought to myself, if he hits me, I'd throw these eggs at him. Then I thought, "Why are these eggs in here anyway."

I got on my hands and knees, sat up in the bed, looked directly at Klyde and said again, "It's going to be okay, I love you!" He leaped towards me, picked up the carton of eggs and threw them at my head. He grabbed me and threw me backward onto the bed.

I jumped up on the bed trying to make a mad dash for the door, but he pulled me down and started socking me. I rolled onto the floor and crawled, pulling away. He threw me aside. I said I was sorry. I begged him not to go. I heard the door open and slam shut. I curled up in a ball and cried. I didn't want him to go, but I was torn because I also felt like a prisoner in my own home.

He came back and beat me again. I managed to get away and run into the bathroom. Klyde banged on the door. He told me if I divorced him, I would be damaged goods and no one would want me.

I called Klyde's friend Pastor G. He was out to dinner with his family. I told him I needed help and explained what happened. Pastor G. asked what I did to provoke him. He caught me off guard. I said, "Excuse me." He repeated, "What did you do to provoke him?"

I never told anyone what was going on, but I couldn't take the blows he was throwing. Pastor G. told me he didn't do it without a reason. I was crying on the phone. I didn't do anything. I hung up and called the police. The police came over, arrested him, and took and him to jail. The judge sentenced him to anger management counseling.

I tried all sorts of things to deal with the abuse. I snuck out once a week and went to the Agape house on Greenfield and Grand River. They had a group session for battered and abused women. I say *snuck* because he didn't know I was getting counseling. I took Jade with me. I was glad they had someone watching the children while we were in therapy.

I commented one day about Klyde lying about his whereabouts. The director told me if I couldn't accept the reason he was giving, I shouldn't ask. But it was no reason to lie to me. I understood the needs of a man are different from that of a woman. I didn't want to be a nag and I wanted Klyde to know I trusted him, so I stopped asking questions that upset him.

I knew the power of words could rip you apart, but they could also make you whole. I had to use words to change my situation. I built myself up in order to become stronger and confident.

Foursome

Dear Lord,

The pleasure Klyde received from the intimate warmth of my body against his... seemed to be the only thing that calmed him. In my endeavors to keep him happy, I pleasured him as often as he wanted, until the day it wasn't enough anymore.

I asked him what else I could do to show him my love. He told one of his fantasies was to have a threesome. I wanted to make my husband happy, so I pleased him the way he wanted, maybe he'd stop the violent outrages and wouldn't stray again. I remembered reading a scripture about the marriage bed being undefiled. So I helped him fulfill his fantasy.

We discussed potential women. I only had one friend I would consider asking and Klyde agreed Charm was a good candidate. So I asked her if she would help fulfill Klyde's fantasy with me. Without hesitation, she said no. "All he's done to you, he treats you like a play toy, not his wife, but you're still trying to please him," she said with a disturbed look. "This is another way for him to have an affair in broad daylight. Right in front of your eyes and you're going along with it. Abigail, what is wrong with you? Think about what you're giving up to please a man."

I heard her, but the only thing on my mind was finding a way to please him and make him happy. Since Charm said no, Klyde asked his friend Tay-Tay if he would have sex with me while Klyde had sex with his wife. Tay-Tay said, yes! But he had to ask his wife Mimi if she would.

A week later, we met at Tay-Tay and Mimi's house to discuss the details. We also discussed who could watch our children, where the best place to have the rendezvous would be, and when the best time would be. Tay-Tay and Mimi's apartment won the vote.

A couple of days later we arrived at their door with a bottle of Jack Daniels and Coke. Klyde was eager to get started. He wasn't a drinker, but he took a couple of sips and handed me the glass. We got undressed, climbed into the king sized bed, and got under the covers.

Klyde wanted to do Mimi first, but she said no, she wanted to do her husband first. Tay-Tay climbed on top of Mimi, but jumped up almost immediately after and went into the next room. He plopped down into a brown leather chair.

As Klyde climbed over me to Mimi I asked what happened. She said he was embarrassed. He started feeling on Mimi. She said, "no, wait, I can't do anything until Tay-Tay and Abigail are doing it too." So Klyde sent me to check on him. I went into the next room, knelt beside him, and asked what happened and if he was ok. He wouldn't say anything. I heard Mimi saying "no, wait. I they're not doing anything." Klyde jumped up and poked his head slightly out the door. He ran back and said, "Yes they are. She's between his legs."

I thought about how badly Klyde must've wanted this to make up a lie. Mimi got up and looked for herself, Klyde behind her peeking over her shoulder. She said, "No, she isn't." She came into the room, sat next to me, and held his hand. She said, "It's okay, baby, I love you!" We all got dressed, and Klyde said we could try it again another time. I didn't say this out loud, but was thinking this would never happen again. I was willing to give myself to another man to please my man.

Come Back Home

Dear Lord,

Lord, what did I get myself into? My daughter was getting older. She kept seeing me get jumped on, hurt, and abused. Klyde was distant from our baby girl. He didn't interact with her or act like he loved her. He acted like he didn't like children. "Why doesn't Dad love me? I see him love you but not me," Jade said. I had to ask him to babysit his little girl. Why was he able to go and come as he pleased, but I had a noose around my neck and he loosened it enough to keep me in his eyesight.

Klyde had eight sisters: Debra, Charlene, Pepper, Lily, Salt, Mary, Kate, and May. Mary spent the night from time to time. They helped me around the house. I was always glad when they came over.

Lily reminded me of myself because she had a laid back personality. She kept to herself, and she stayed in her room. I had a special place in my heart for her. You'd never find her in the middle of the mess. I felt close to all of his little sisters. I felt as though they were my flesh and blood. Mary was a little princess and a joy to be around. Pepper spent the night last night. Usually when they came over, Klyde didn't hit me, but this time was different.

Klyde told me whenever I had an issue with him to let him know. I sat on the bed looking down. He asked me what was wrong. I told him he scared me. He turned around as if to say something, but instead he drew back his hand and with a closed fist socked me. I ran into the living room. He punched me in the face. Grabbed me by the hair and threw me against the wall. Jade grabbed my ankle and wouldn't let go.

Pepper tried to grab her and pull her away. I knew it would only get worse if she let go. Jade wouldn't let go of my ankle, to my surprise Klyde swung violently with a belt, slashing me across my back and hitting Jade too.

I knelt down to cover her. Jade was screaming, "Daddy stop, please stop!" I stood with her in my arms and tried to run to the door. He shoved me. I stumbled and fell. As I fell I released my hold of Jade. Pepper ran over and ripped her off me. I curled up in the corner while Klyde continued to beat me with a belt. I yelled out, "I'm sorry, I won't do it again." I didn't know what I was sorry for, but saying I wouldn't do it again made him stop.

Jade ran over to me crying, saying, "I'm sorry, Mommy!" I hugged Jade and put a sweet tart necklace around her neck and told her it was going to be okay. Klyde left me lying on the floor and took his sister home. Pepper didn't tell him to stop; she didn't try to help me. I was embarrassed for her to see me like that. Why didn't she try to help? Maybe she thought it was normal behavior. Had she seen him do this before? Or was she in shock and didn't know what to do.

I couldn't stay in this type of environment. The best way to describe him is Dr. Jekyell and Mr Hyde. What was I teaching my little girl? I had to run away. I cleaned myself up, went to the police station, and made a police report. I called a domestic violence women's shelter to see if they had a bed available. I packed a bag and Jade and I caught the bus to the shelter.

This was the third time in a domestic violence shelter. I had a room to myself with a twin sized bed and a dresser. Jade and I said our prayers, thanking God for his grace, mercy, and keeping power. We then laid our heads on the pillow and went to sleep.

As I drifted off, I thought about the message I was sending to my daughter staying in this abusive relationship. This was not the life I want for her. At the shelter, I woke at 5 a.m. to make breakfast, along with a few other women in residence. Our duties changed weekly. Even though we lived in a shelter, we also worked regular jobs. We were trying to start our lives over in a safe environment. I caught the bus to and from Mercy Health Services. I had a curfew and we were sworn to secrecy to keep the location safe.

The shelter was a way of escape for me. I could not keep going on like it was. But every time I left, he begged for my forgiveness. I really wanted my marriage to work, so much my soul ached. I was married, for better or worse. When was the *better* going to come? I didn't want to die trying to make it better, but I wanted my marriage.

Whenever I left, Klyde acted better. I thought maybe this time it would last longer. He always told me he wouldn't do it again. He said he needed me to come back home and told me how beautiful I was. When I dropped off Jade at my mother's-in-law house. Beatrice told me Pepper and Klyde told her what happened. She went on to say if this happened again to let the baby go so she wouldn't get hurt. She told me I should apologize to Pepper. I said, "What about me?"

All she could say was I was wrong for holding Jade in my arms and I want to make sure Jade's safe. I didn't argue with older people, so I apologized to Pepper and agreed not to do it again.

Klyde picked up Jade sometimes. When she came back, she asked, "If Daddy gives you flowers will you go back? Daddy told me he loves you and wants you to come back home." I was not convinced he'd changed. We talked about a few things and he let me go to the house to get some of my things. I found a slew of love letters. Klyde was working at a credit agency in Bloomfield off Orchard Lake. I found out he'd been dating a lady who worked at a modeling agency on 8 Mile road. She wrote him love letters and tried to convert him into the Muslim faith. My sister, Soni, told me rumors were going around at her job that Klyde was sleeping with her. The crazy thing was I felt everyone knew more information about my relationship than me. It was rumored, the lady got her hair done by my cousin LaWanna.

My cousin owned a hair salon off 7 Mile and Wyoming. I went to the hairdresser and asked if I could speak with her. She took me into her office. She told me the girl would come in to get her hair done and she talked about her boyfriend Klyde.

She went on to tell her she was the one who picked up Jade's birthday cake and picked up a gold plated rose for me. She goes on and on about how she loves him, but he always brings me up, the girl says.

"She sounds obsessed," my cousin said. "But it sounds like he still loves you."

I had a conversation with Klyde. I told him if I came back he had to cut off all communication with her. He said, "But I'm in love with her too. I love both of you." It was worse than I thought. She had his mind and his heart. "It's not about the sex," he said. "I can't turn it off and don't know what to do." But, in the end, he said he would break it off because he wanted his marriage. So I came back.

He was treating me better. I had no proof he stopped talking to her, but I did have faith. I trusted he ended the relationship.

Male Exotic Dancers

I was desperately trying to find a form of happiness and entertainment. My friend asked if I wanted to go Watts Mozambigue Lounge, a male exotic dance club. I was curious and wanted to but scared to ask Klyde if I could go. So I made up a story a few of my girlfriends were getting together for her birthday and going out to Friday's for dinner.

He said I could go, but I had to be back by 11 p.m. I didn't know what to wear, so I wore a pair of slacks and a shirt. We sat at one of the tables not far from the stage.

I was excited, embarrassed and terrified all at the same time. I was nervous and scared to look at them but tempted. I glanced up, and all I saw were half naked men stripping down to a piece of material wrapped around their private parts. Some had bells hanging from them others had tassels.

I was terrified for several reasons. I thought what if they start grinding in front of me. What if his "Surprise Package" accidentally brushed up against me? How would I handle it? Would I scream? Would I have a nervous laugh? Would I want jump up? Would I want to grab him?

I had never seen a stripper nor did I dream I'd see one live and in person. I looked around noticing how muscular and sexy these guys where. I got more relaxed, and the night went on. This was the most fun I had in a long time. One of the male dancers did come over to me and started bumping and grinding. I was so embarrassed my body went numb and sat there.

I heard women shouting out, "Woo, baby!" He whipped his shirt off and threw it to the floor. He was doing a strip tease, waving his body starting with his head then traveled down to his legs. It didn't take long before his pants came off.

With my hands over my face, praying, Lord, Jesus let this man go away with all of his stuff hanging out. I began to panic; he backed up into my lap, laid back and started grinding my leg. My friend next to me shouted, "Go ahead," while I tried to catch my breath. I slipped a couple of dollar bills into his G-string hoping he'd go away.

It felt like it went on for hours, but it was only a few minutes. Eventually, the music stopped and he picked up his clothes and exited the room. I sat, trying to process what happened. Out of nowhere he reappeared and struck up a conversation with me. I was caught off guard and hoping he'd go away, but it felt nice I was noticed. He asked for my number and I gave it to him.

I received a call from the male dancer asking to me meet me after work. Later I found out he was shot and in the hospital. Little did I know Klyde knew about the male dancer. He confronted me about having an affair. He knew quite a bit about that night at the male strip club.

I did talk to him on the phone once, but I tried to deny any of it was true. I asked a friend to cover for me, but she knew how crazy Klyde was and wanted no part of it. He wasn't worried too much because the guy was in the hospital. He told me he had people watching me, and I'd better be careful.

It didn't matter where I went, he had spies everywhere reporting back to him where I was. I felt like I was in a maze waiting for the alligator to come around the next corner.

Whenever I needed a peace of mind, to feel secure and whole, I would recite Psalm 23:1. I called it the Blueberry Prayer.

Blueberry Prayer
Psalm 23:1-6

The Lord is my shepherd;

    I shall not want.

    He maketh me to lie down in green pastures:

    he leadeth me beside the still waters.

    He restoreth my soul:

    he leadeth me in the paths of righteousness for

    his name's sake.

    Yea, though I walk through the valley of the

shadow of death,

    I will fear no evil: for thou art with me;

thy rod and thy staff they comfort me.

    Thou preparest a table before me in the

presence of mine enemies:

    Thou anointest my head with oil; my cup

runneth over.

    Surely, goodness and mercy shall follow me all

the days of my life: and I will dwell in the house of

the Lord forever.

Chapter 6
Tears of Pain

Dear Lord,

One perfectly calm morning, Klyde and I drove down Southfield Freeway. He asked why I didn't have on the red lipstick he liked. I told him I really didn't like red lipstick, and pink looked better on me. Before I could blink, he tightened his jaws, gritted his teeth, and slung his arm across my face. He hit me in the nose with a bottle. I was terrified of what might happen next.

After months of peace, I thought, not again. I was not going to take this anymore. I looked over my right shoulder, opened the car door, and jumped out while he was driving 25 mph. I rolled on the ground while oncoming traffic was coming, but quickly got out of the way. I got up, limping and wiping my fingertips across my eyes, pushing away tears. As I limped with cuts and bruises on my legs and arms, I glanced over my shoulder to see if he had pulled over. He didn't.

Cars started honking, people yelled out their car windows asking if I was okay. Complete strangers seemed to care more about me than my own husband. I nodded yes and kept walking, not wanting anyone to see me. Klyde kept beeping me on my pager, but I didn't respond. Even though this guy was obviously crazy, I didn't want my family to find out he was abusing me.

So I walked and walked trying to figure out what to do. I walked to my Uncle Leroy's house in Oak Park to see if I could hang out over there for a while. I stayed until my friend Charm picked me up. When she looked at me, she told me I deserved better, and I needed to get out before things got worse.

After I got to Charm's house, I called Klyde's mother's house to check on Jade. She told me Klyde told her he didn't mean to hit me. Then she put him on the phone and he tried to tell me he was throwing a bottle out the window and the wind blew and made him accidentally hit me in the face. I didn't let him convince me it was an accident. I was there, it happened to me. I slammed the phone down and spent the night at my friend's house.

I went back to the craziness the following day like it was a revolving door. I thought he would change after we got married. The horrible thing was I started to notice I was struggling to bond with Jade. I was withdrawn and preoccupied trying to stay mentality sane and keep up with working and day-to-day chores. I felt somewhat tuned-out and emotionless to things around me. I wanted so desperately to have a good relationship with her. She had already been through so much. She'd seen her mother get verbally and physically abused and been in shelters for battered and abused women and children. These are things a child should never have to encounter.

I was also terrified the information I received about how to care for her was wrong, or did I misunderstand. I was told not to hold her, to let her cry; you don't want to spoil her. I couldn't find a rulebook on how to raise a child, each child is unique. I wanted to raise her right, so I listened. But I was afraid I damaged her. My baby needed me to build her, feel my warmth and love for her. Feeling nurtured, loved, and secure was something every child needed when they entered this world.

How was holding her going to spoil her? What is the right amount of holding time? It didn't help for her to see me get slapped around either. When people say things like, "a child is better off growing up in a two-parent household," I wondered why. This statement should be exempt when abuse is involved. I wondered if Jade knew what was going on and if she'd think this was normal for a woman to get jumped on.

I started looking up scriptures in the bible on how to be more submissive and kinder. I felt I had to become a better wife and mother. I needed to fix what I was doing wrong. I was so unhappy, depressed, and stressed and I needed to change.

Les Brown once said, "I <u>believe</u> that life is a journey, often difficult and sometimes incredibly cruel, but we are well …."

Life has definitely been a journey for me and cruel. I didn't know what tomorrow held, but I did know I needed to find some type of relief and then we will be well.

Love Affair

Dear Lord,

I have sinned. I was no better than Klyde. I was so tired of being mistreated. The sight of Klyde made me angry and frustrated. He cheated on me and made me feel guilty about it. Sex with him was like exercise. I was doing all sorts of things to please him, but no matter what I did I couldn't please him or do anything right.

I found out Nick, my friend since the third grade, was coming to town. He was tall and slender, with an athletic build, deep dimples, and a gorgeous smile. He had dark wavy hair, and had an exotic tropical feel. I wanted, no, I needed to feel love. To be around someone I knew loved me unconditionally. I had to see him. He always made me smile. I needed to smile. I needed a big loving bear hug from my dearest friend.

I met up with him. I felt like I was sad and broken. I didn't express my problems to him, but knew something was wrong. He held me in his arms. It was comforting and soothing to be close to him and feel the love. He excited me and made my heart smile. I raised my head up from his chest and he looked down. His lips met my forehead with a light kiss then they met mine.

I thought, "I'm married," but the thought disappeared in the warmth of his arms and his touch. His smile was like a dose of medicine to get me through the day. I felt a sense of relief and a moment of peace. I was willing and able to feel what I needed. I couldn't blame it on alcohol. I knew fully what I was doing. He comforted me and I wanted him to.

Then reality set in. I was disappointed in myself. I never intended to be in the arms of another man. I was no better than Klyde. I knew what I was doing.

I felt I had to tell Klyde. I couldn't be in a marriage with secrets. This would have eaten at me forever. While lying in bed, I asked Klyde if I could make a confession without him getting upset and judging me. He told me to go ahead, so I told him what I did. Surprisingly, he didn't get upset. In fact, he thanked me for being honest with him, hugged me, and went to sleep.

I thought this was strange, but I told myself he must've accepted the fact he'd been treating me wrong and now he understood I loved him and I was heartbroken. I fell asleep on the edge of the bed wondering what he was really thinking.

I vowed to myself not to ever let anger or betrayal affect who I am and what I stood for.

Klyde's Big Idea

Dear Lord,

Klyde woke up one morning and told me he wanted to be a concert promoter. He wanted to throw a concert with Marvin Gay and wanted the headliner to be Two Live Crew. They were a hip-hop group from Miami, Florida who had some kind of sexual theme in all their music.

It was a bit raunchy. "Sex sales," Klyde said. But he needed investors. I told him he should try to find a group of investors in the industry who help young people get started because if something went wrong it would be part of the business. Investors take risks. We calculated all the costs entailed in putting together a concert.

Of course instead of asking investors, he asked his father. He pitched his dream to his dad and his dad gave him $10,000.

At this time, I was pregnant with our second child. So when it was time to go to New Orleans, he thought he should go alone. I was off work and wanted to go, but I was also pregnant and wanted what was best for the baby. To say the least, the concert flopped and his dad's money went down the tube. The loss came from the lack of ticket sales.

When Klyde came back he told me one of his ex-girlfriends said he had gotten her pregnant when he was living in Baton Rouge. She had a little girl and didn't tell him. He went on to say everyone thought the little girl looked like him. But, he also said he didn't think it was his and she didn't want anything from him.

Later, I was in the basement looking at old bank statements when I stumbled upon a folder with information from the Two Live crew Concert, the one Klyde promoted. Hanging out of the folder was a picture of Klyde and a woman at a club. Thoughts ran through my mind. I wondered if he'd slept with her. I figured it was his other baby's mama. I thought about what his reaction might be if the photo came up missing, but I didn't care. I tore the picture up in little pieces. I heard him come in the side door so I hid the pieces and ran upstairs.

He sat his things down and went downstairs

where he found what was left of the picture I tore up. He yelled upstairs for me to come down. I had a feeling he knew what I did, but when he asked me what happened to the picture I told him I didn't know. I asked, "What was it a picture of?" He said someone had taken a picture of him and the lady who said she had his baby. I asked him why he had it and if he slept with her. He got angry and started yelling. He hit the wall and left.

I didn't understand why he'd get so angry if she didn't mean anything to him. When he came back he didn't mention it. He got in the bed and went to sleep. His reaction answered my question.

What I'm Thankful For

Dear Lord,

My little girl spoke today in church about what she was thankful for. My darling, little girl said: "I'm thankful for my mother because she takes good care of me. She feeds me and takes me to school. When I didn't do a good job cleaning my room, she would do it for me. That's why I am thankful for my mother."

Jade enjoyed going to church. She took notes and danced on the youth praise team. She touched my heart in a way only a daughter could. Klyde and I usually discussed punishment whenever Jade was disobedient. He thought when she got into trouble she shouldn't be able to participate in any church events. Praise team was one of them.

I couldn't see what taking away a church event would teach her. Church was a positive thing and never should be a punishment. The problem was she didn't not have any extra activities or toys she played with to take away.

So instead of taking praise team completely away, he agreed to have her sit out one event.

I loved to see Jade being a part of the church and enjoying it. I started to appreciate motherhood. It was hard for so long. Starting a family so young and getting married, taking care of the entire household was overwhelming. I thought I was ready to be a wife and mother, but I was not prepared to become an adult so soon. I will say being a mother had brought me some sense of peace. When I looked into Jade's magical eyes smiling back at me, my heart fluttered with joy. I was so glad I made the decision to keep her.

New Edition

Dear Lord,

I was eight months pregnant when I started having labor pains. I was working at Mercy Health Services filing papers when all of a sudden I felt like I was having the worst menstrual cramp I'd ever experienced. Combined with the feeling someone was stabbing me in the stomach. I slowly walked to my supervisor's office and told her I was going into labor.

She had one of my coworkers drive me to the hospital. I was in Farmington Hills, but my doctor was in Pontiac, Michigan 30 minutes away. After getting checked into the hospital and examined, the doctor determined it was too early for me to deliver. He felt the baby was not fully developed, so he stopped the labor and put me on bed rest.

I wanted to be closer to my mom and I would get the most help if I stayed with her. After being on bed rest for a month, nothing was happening. I was still pregnant and it didn't seem like the baby wanted to come out anymore. So, I started looking up things to help me go into labor faster. Mixing castor oil with juice and walking was one of them, so I tried it. I walked around my mother's house until I couldn't walk anymore.

I went to the hospital without a labor pain in sight. I was tired of carrying such a heavy load. The doctor examined me and I was only dilated two centimeters. I needed to be at least ten centimeters in order to deliver the baby. I asked the doctor if he could induce my labor. I was already two weeks past my due date, my water hadn't broken, and contractions weren't coming fast enough. I started drinking lots of water and walking in order to help the process along.

Eventually, the contractions came. My cervix dilated from two to six centimeters, and contractions were fifteen to twenty minutes apart and lasted sixty to ninety seconds. The contractions worsened, but my water wouldn't break. Finally, the doctor decided to break my water. The labor pain was much more painful than I remembered. I had a lot of cramping under my stomach. Sharp pains shot through my body. The pain started at the top of my back and went down to my lower back. As time went on, the contractions grew more intense and closer together. It was like I was a wind up doll and my insides were being twisted, pulled, and squeezed.

When the pain became almost unbearable, it was time to push. I thought when I pushed it was going to feel better, like when I delivered Jade. Not so, it felt like I was being ripped apart at first. Eager to get the baby out, I gave one last push. The doctor spanked the baby's bottom and it cried. The doctor held him up and said, "It's a boy!"

I started to name him Raphael Armani because I liked both designers and I thought the names sounded cool together, but I decided I wanted a name that started with a J like Jade's so I named him Ja'vian.

Jade helped me so much with her little brother. Whenever I needed her, she was there. She would get diapers when he needed to be changed, after he finished his bottle she wiped his mouth, and she helped me pick out his clothes. But as he grew she became resentful and jealous of her little brother. She felt Ja'vian was getting more attention than she was.

Jade turned three a few months ago, but she wanted me to pick her up and put her brother down. I explain to her mommy's back hurts and she is a big girl and doesn't need to sit on mommy's lap anymore. I felt like it was time for Jade to grow up and share the attention. I wanted Ja'vian to experience love and affection from birth. I didn't realize Jade still needed it too because she didn't get it when she needed it the most. Sibling rivalry soon set in.

One afternoon, while driving down 7 Mile Road, I looked through the rear view mirror and Jade leaned over and grabbed her baby brother's arm and sunk her teeth into it. My first thought was to bite her back, but I remembered you should not whoop your child when you're angry because you might unintentionally hurt them. So I took a deep breath to calm down. I showed her the teeth marks on his arm and explained to her that her behavior was unacceptable.

"Never bite your little brother or anyone else," I said. Then I told her I was going to show her what her brother felt when she bit him so she would never do it again. I took her wrist, rolled up her sleeve, put my mouth on the thickness of her arm, and bit into her in a way she would remember. I showed her the teeth marks on her arm and said, "Look, it's the same, and it hurts the same." I told her I loved her and gave her a hug.

My mom told me early on I shouldn't have any more children. Jade required a lot of attention and if I had more children it would take away from her. I didn't understand. I thought I gave her a lot of attention. I didn't see what my mom saw.

Hitch Hiker

Dear Lord,

Even though Jade was still little, I took her to work on mother-daughter day so I could spend more time with her. She was younger than most of the other children, but she was well behaved. I received compliments all the time on how well behaved she was. Of course, as a mother, you see only the flaws and want to make sure everything was perfect.

After Jade came to work with me a couple of years in a row, my supervisor Mrs. JB fell in love with her, and asked to be her Godmother. JB was a happy but stern person. I enjoyed having her as my supervisor and loved the fact she wanted to be Jade's Godmother.

One day I was on my way home from work when the front axle broke on our car. When I got home, I didn't feel well. It wasn't like me to have anything hold me down, but when I woke up I felt heaviness in my body. I was mentally and physically drained. I never called in sick, but this day seemed like a good day to do it.

I told Klyde I didn't feel well and needed to stay

home and rest, but he made me get up and get dressed. Since my car was broken he dropped me off. When JB arrived, she looked at me and asked if I was okay. I told her I was a little under the weather, but I would be okay. Within a few hours, my mind drifted and my body followed and became weak.

I couldn't lift my hands to key in the figures. I felt like a screw kept loosening as the day went on. I stood and stumbled. "Enough," I said to myself. I couldn't take it anymore. I asked JB if I could have the rest of the day off.

Getting home was a challenge. My family lived forty-five minutes away and they would have asked me too many questions. Calling Klyde for a ride was not an option. He'd be upset if I went home. So I started walking. I turned off the main road to avoid being seen. I tried to jump over the guardrail, but my leg caught on the rail and ripped my pantyhose from my ankle to my thigh. A driver saw me struggling to walk and I tripped a couple of times.

Then a stranger pulled over and asked me if I was okay and if I needed help. I said I was fine, but he saw rips in my panty hose, blood dripping from my leg, and I was limping. He said, "I see you're hurt. I can take you where you need to go." I told him I didn't take rides from strangers. He could be a mass murderer. But I already felt dead inside and I lived twenty miles away. It would take me hours to get home. He introduced himself, handed me a business card, and told me he was here to help and he wouldn't hurt me. Exhausted, I got into the car.

The entire time I was in the car, I thought if Klyde knew I got in the car with a stranger he'd flip out. When I first got into the car, I looked around the back seat, checked the door handles and locks on the door. He asked me questions, but I gave him very little information. I prayed all the way home. When we pulled up to my house, I was hoping Klyde was not there. But it was as if he knew I was on the way home. As I reached for the knob, he snatched the door open.

Klyde immediately started questioning me about the man dropping me off, and why I wasn't at work. I told him exactly what happened, how I felt before I left the house, him making me go to work, and the stranger offering to take me home because he saw me struggling to walk." Are you stupid, what's wrong with you," Klyde said. "Do you have a death wish? You're worthless and pitiful! I can't believe you did this to me. I'm gonna call the pastor and tell him what you did."

I said, "I'm sorry, but I needed to come home, I'm not feeling well." Then I handed him a business card. He snatched it out of my hand and I said I was sorry again. "Sorry, was for SORRY people," he said. "I'm tired of you always saying you're sorry. If you don't want me to call you *sorry* stop saying it and say you *apologize*." He called the man who kindly took me home, questioned him, and told him not to ever see me again and slammed the phone down.

Then he called Pastor Wyndam over to speak with me. He came to the house and sat in the living room on our large comfy cream sofa facing the fireplace. As I sat next to him, he explained how dangerous getting into a car with a stranger was. I listened intensely to what he had to say. Tears swelled up in my eyes.

I told Pastor Wyndam he didn't understand what I was going through. My life wasn't important and I didn't care whether I lived or died. After he ministered and prayed with me, I told him I understood it was dangerous and it wouldn't happen again.

Psalms 23:4

Even tough I walk
through the darkest vally,
I will fear no evil,
for you are with me;
your rod and your staff,
they comfort me.

Chapter 7
Plain Mad

Dear Lord,

Sunday morning, Pastor Wyndam taught on family and what the wife's responsibilities were. When the pastor said a wife should cook, Klyde spoke out with a loud "Amen!" When the pastor said she should respect her husband, he shouted out again, "Amen!"

This went on throughout the entire service. I was so embarrassed. He made it seem as though I didn't cook, clean, or take care of him. It amazed me that he reacted this way when he spends most Sundays hitting, slapping, or stomping me, but I still treat him with respect.

Klyde started on me right after church. He started yelling, finding fault in everything I did. I sat quietly while he ranted because my mother taught me it takes two to argue and to never argue in front of the children. I knew my mother was right. He asked me a question and I answered it with the shortest response I could think of, but my answers were not good enough. As we approached

Greenfield and Schoolcraft, right before the bridge, he told me to get out and walk home. Greenfield was a busy road and too dangerous to even break down in, let alone walk. I had no choice but to get out because I didn't want to cause a scene in front of the children and I definitely didn't want him to hit me. I looked back at Jade and Ja'vian, got out of the car, and started walking.

While I walked home, I was hoping no one from church would see me. When I got home, I hugged and kissed Jade and Ja'vian. I told them I loved them. I fed, bathed, and got them dressed for bed.

I knew there would come another day when Klyde would do something mean. I had to build myself up and get stronger if I was going to stay with him. I felt an obligation to stay married, not because of the wedding vows, but for the children and my quest to break the generational curse of broken homes.

A few months after the bridge incident, I got mad. He loved to socialize and brag about what he was doing or what he had, usually he mingle while I sat in the car and waited but one day after church I didn't feel like waiting. I told him I was tired and wanted to go home. After about thirty minutes, I put both children in the car and left him standing in the parking lot with all his family surrounding him.

I didn't know where I got the courage to take off and leave him. It might have been the message preached about how a wife should treat her husband when Klyde decided to yell out "Amen, amen!"

I waited at home and prepared for an argument. Klyde's mother dropped him off. He was shocked I even pulled such a move, but so was I. I was tired of being afraid, getting pushed around, mistreated, and abused. "For God gave us a spirit not of fear..." 2 Timothy 1:7. He said I better not ever embarrass him again or I would be sorry. I knew not to say anything. He grabbed the keys and left.

How did I get here? I was pregnant with our third child. I had contracted a sexually transmitted disease during each pregnancy. I was so naïve. Klyde convinced me I had a virus in my body that developed over time. He was so convincing and persuasive. I believed him.

I didn't want to be "left high and dry," as my dad would say. Once, Klyde walked by the hallway closet where I kept my some of my clothes. I accidently left the door cracked open. As he opened it he inspected the bottom of the closet and he found a bottle of Humphrey 11 pills. He knew exactly what they were because I bought them after I got pregnant with my second child. If I took enough of them, it could cause a miscarriage. He called the pastor over to talk some sense into me. I told the pastor I wished God would take this baby out and give it to someone else. I felt so alone.

Counseling for us was non-stop. We stopped seeking marriage counseling with the pastor so whenever we had any issues, we'd counseled with a married couple, Dirk and Louise, in their home. They were a nice couple and did their best to help us, but I was confused at times. I thought I was losing my mind. But I had to keep it together. When I died, I wanted Jade to be strong enough to take care of herself and not end up like me.

This time, I decided to leave not because of physical abuse, but mental abuse. I was tired of being mistreated and disrespected. After repeated incidents at the beauty salon, I asked Klyde to quit and find another job. I caught women brushing up against him on purpose, slapping him on his butt, or placing their hands between his butt cheeks and gripping his butt.

I couldn't believe he had the nerve to deny what I saw when I was looking right at him. If this was happening right in front of my face, who knew what was going on when I wasn't around. I found myself popping up at the shop like a jealous woman, and I was not the jealous type.

I felt like I was losing myself. Sometimes I felt so panicked. It's like the feeling you get when on an airplane and the door shuts. Suddenly you realize you're on a plane packed tightly. You're trapped in a small metal tube about to launch into space.

I waited until he left and packed the entire two-bedroom, one bathroom house. We didn't have much. I took only the necessities:

my personal items, the children's clothes, the TV, and radio. I put it all in the car.

Before I was able to load the last few items, Klyde came home. My older brother Tony, who was six feet tall and slim, was in town from Florida. He was helping me. "Get off my porch and don't come in my house," Klyde said. "This is my sister's house too," Tony said. "Isn't she paying the bills? She doesn't want to be here and I'm not leaving." Then Klyde pulled out a gun and put it to my brother's head.

My brother Tony stood with no fear, while my little brother Jerome watched. Tony said, "If you're going to pull the trigger, then go ahead. You know where I come from. I am not afraid of you. I'm helping my sister. She does not want to be here. So step aside."

Klyde cocked the gun and stood in silence. He glanced over and saw our daughter looking up at him, then put the gun away. We finished loading the car and drove off. Klyde didn't say anything at the time. He didn't have to. I moved in with my brother Al.

Public Display of Abuse

Dear Lord,

The day after the move, I went to my office at Mercy Health Services. I was tired from the move, so I was taking a break in the reflection room when a coworker told me my husband was here looking for me. With a shiver in my voice I said, "He's here?" I immediately got nervous, but I didn't want to share my personal business with her so I remained calm. I walked into the claims department where he'd been looking for me. I asked him to follow me into the atrium away from my coworkers.

As I walked ahead of him, he asked me why I took the radio. I started walking faster so no one would hear us. He said again, with fury, "You took the radio and the TV! You left me with nothing. Why did you take the radio?" I told him I paid for the radio and gave him the money to give to his mother.

He immediately became belligerent. He grabbed me and flung me into the bushes. He said, "You did not have to take the radio and the TV." I tried to get up, but he socked me and pushed me back down. I started yelling, "Help, please somebody help me!" He kicked, stomped, and punched me repeatedly. Then he picked me up again and dropped me. I tried my best to get away, but everywhere I ran he was there blocking me.

Klyde continued to chase me throughout the atrium while my coworkers stood around and watched like deer in headlights. I have some idea why they didn't help. They were all women, probably in shock, and didn't want to get hit or involved. Everyone on the first floor and some from the second ran into the atrium to witness the beating. They all looked frightened and helpless. A two hundred pound hulk pouncing on a frail hundred pound woman would scare anyone. He was a weak man with low self-esteem issues and a touch of the crazies.

Louise, my unborn baby's Godmother's voice rumbled out, "Klyde, Klyde STOP, Klyde stop," she said. She yelled it many times before the roar of her voice finally penetrated his ears. He stopped and looked around. Security came to escort him out, but he ran. I was taken to the hospital and checked for scrapes and bruises and to make sure the baby was okay. I was in my first trimester. When the police questioned me, I told them I wanted to file a restraining order against him and press charges.

Klyde turned himself in a couple days later. He was charged with domestic abuse and the court ordered him to counseling and community service. After the attack I was embarrassed and didn't want to face my co-workers. I didn't know what was causing Klyde to destroy his family.

I went to church every Sunday and attended bible class on Tuesdays. I did my best to listen to what God was telling me, but I hadn't seen anywhere in the bible that talked about abuse. He committed adultery with people in and out of the church. I did not want to ever forgive him for what he did to me.

What I didn't understand was how or why he could be so violent toward me. To my knowledge he didn't smoke or drink. But, he once wrote a poem about a crack head; as if he knew how they felt. He must be insane to beat me up in front of everyone, right?

I couldn't see how I could stay married to a crazy person. I remembered the last time I left.

He told me if I ever left him again I couldn't come back. This time I didn't have to worry about him trying to get me back.

My family was furious when they found out Klyde beat me up at work. They called him a coward and a few other choice words. They wanted him to feel my pain. A few of my family members and friends asked me if I wanted them to put a contract hit out on him. Even my dad, who never liked him and didn't want me to marry him, said he knew people who could break him down and take him out.

My brother told me: "Nod your head and I'll know what to do." But this was the father of my children. I didn't want to see him hurt or my children to be without a father. However, there was a part of me that wanted him to feel my pain. I wasn't sure what I should do, so I took a leave of absence from work.

After Klyde's sneak attack, I was afraid to stay in Michigan. So I moved to Tallahassee, Florida with my brother Tony to figure out what I wanted to do. I was searching to recreate and rediscover myself. I filled out job applications and went on interviews.

We went to a flea market looking for camera equipment. As we walked toward the entrance I looked up into a large tree. A small light green lizard peeked through the leaves. I'd never seen a real lizard so I lingered a bit. It was small, but long and slender. As I walked underneath the tree, the lizard jumped onto my chest. I screamed, jumped around, and screamed some more. I felt it moving around. I kept shaking, but the lizard clung to my clothes. So I started undressing right then and there. It fell off of me and squirmed away. "Welcome to Florida," my brother said.

By month end, Klyde threatened to tell the police I kidnapped the children, so I went back to Detroit. My brother drove me from Florida. Even though I was embarrassed to go back to work, it was a stable job and paid well.

My co-workers stared at me and seemed concerned, but no one asked questions. I continued to work and tried to act like everything was normal. It wasn't everyday people witnessed a co-worker being attacked. They were traumatized. I heard a few people sought counseling after that. I prayed to God to help me through the hurt and the shame.

Single Lady

Dear Lord,

Over the year I thought a lot about my future. I prayed and meditated about healing my marriage even though I thought it was over for good. Especially when he didn't think he did anything wrong.

I counseled with Sister Naomi from church. She reached out to me after sensing something was wrong. It took me a minute to open up to her. I didn't tell her about the physical abuse, but we spoke a lot about how I should respond to Klyde when he gets angry. She taught me how to interact with Klyde; what to say and what not to say. It really helped to keep the peace and I didn't seem to make Klyde so angry.

My main focus was figuring out how I was going to survive without him. I never wanted to move back home after I left, but for the duration of my pregnancy, it was where I found myself. In order to grow and move forward I had to distance myself from Klyde so I limited all communication with him.

After accepting the fact we weren't going to be together, I reached into myself and find the strength to keep it together and be strong for my daughter, son and, unborn child. The first few months were the hardest. I desperately needed to fall into the arms of my mom, but I didn't want her to know how much pain I was really in. I didn't want to burden my sister either. Tears would flow. The more I tried to stop them, the more they came.

I started seeing a therapist to help me with my emotions. She was the cushiony grandmother type, warm and nurturing. We instantly bonded. I consulted the bible daily for understanding. I had to figure it out myself, and I didn't want to be influenced by anyone. I tried to block out the pain by keeping busy.

As time went on my mind started getting stronger. I thought less about Klyde and more about my children and myself. It seemed as though my self-esteem was rebuilding. I saw a lot of me in Jade and I wanted her to see more than what was there. She was the joy in my life. I would sacrifice my life for her.

I wanted to get a promotion at work and become a claims examiner, but I needed training. I signed up for a medical terminology course at Marygrove College. I also signed Jade up for piano lessons there. Maybe she'd like it so much she'd become the next Beethoven. I kept all the notes so I could teach myself.

Every day, I picked up Jade after school and caught the bus to the college. Her class was over before mine so I took her with me. She sat behind me playing with a baby doll. The professor asked a question once and Jade raised her hand and answered the question. The class laughed and was impressed by her response and so was I, but at the same time, I felt like a horrible mother. I'd always been hard and stern with Jade because I wanted to make sure she grew up to be a strong woman who didn't have to depend on a man.

I taught Jade to feel free to express herself to me because I couldn't express myself with Mom growing up. So whenever I got a note from Jade it made the pain go away for a moment. She wrote: "I stand for many grateful things God made. I stand for you. I stand for God's child. I stand for courage. I stand for my bother Ja'vian and Mom. I stand for God because God is a healer and our father. He's the greatest person I know. I also stand for respect because I give respect, I am respect. All I give is respect most of the time. But I try my hardest to be good all the time."

I dropped Jade and Ja'vian at the sitters and shortly after felt a bit off. The day before, we'd gone to the movies and I had backaches throughout the entire movie, but was fine afterwards. When I was at work I noticed I was having lots of Braxton Hicks contractions and I got a bit nervous.

I drank a big glass of water, but the contractions seemed to get worse. I didn't want to make a big deal out of it and scare my co-workers, but I told my supervisor and was taken to the hospital. Work and me going into labor seemed to be a common denominator. When I got to the hospital, they put me on a monitor to track my contractions and checked the baby's heart rate.

I was not complaining about going into labor early because I did not want a large baby coming out of me. The last one wasn't easy. I was given a shot and after the contractions slowed they sent me home with strict orders to stay on bed rest until it was time to deliver. Three weeks of bed rest had me so bored. And

I was tired of carrying such a heavy load. I watched TV, but mostly I wrote in my journal and napped.

I decided I wanted to have the baby now, so I walked and walked until I got tired and felt faint labor pains, but nothing serious and far apart. I called my mom at work. I told her I thought I was going into labor, but not to worry and there was no need to rush home. I sat, but was restless and soon after, the contractions got closer. I still didn't think it was serious, but I drove myself to Providence Hospital in Southfield just in case.

I was reluctant to call Klyde, but I did anyway. I got to the labor and delivery room and got undressed. The doctor checked my cervix and said the baby hadn't come down enough yet. The contractions weren't close enough, so I walked the halls of the hospital and drank lots of water. I even thought about jumping up and down.

Eventually the contractions came closer together and the pain got worse, but my water hadn't broken. The doctor checked my cervix and I was six centimeters dilated. The pain was intense, so I grabbed the guardrail and shook it rigorously. My doctor was not available to deliver my child so another doctor did. The doctor asked me if I wanted an epidural. This time I said, yes!

By the time Klyde got there I was eight centimeters dilated. My back was in serious pain. I had him massage it. I didn't yell, but I gritted my teeth and said, "I don't ever want to do this again."

When it was time to deliver, the doctor asked if I wanted an episiotomy. "If I need one," I said. So, he didn't give me one. As the baby's head came through, I felt my skin tearing and burning. I said, "Why didn't you give me an episiotomy." He said it was too late. I yelled with every push. The baby came. Another boy. But wait, there's more. The after birth was horribly painful! It was worse than the delivery of the baby.

The doctor pushed and pushed on my stomach like he was trying to kill me, but if all the afterbirth didn't come out, I would have died. I tore so badly. I needed 12 stiches. After two deliveries, I have to say the third was the most painful, even with medication. I was relieved it was over and when I looked at the new baby Ja'von, it made the pain worth it.

Having a third child by a man who was no

longer in my life was frustrating. I was married, but living single. Two days after the birth of little Ja'von I moved back in with my mother. After carrying the baby for nine months and going through labor, I was quite exhausted. I had to admit I was grateful to my mom for taking care of me during the pregnancy and for weeks after giving birth.

My mother relieved me of all responsibilities other than feeding the baby and taking care of myself. I was able to sleep when the baby slept. Sometimes it was for long periods of time and other times not so much, but every minute helped.

Six weeks after Ja'von was born Klyde wanted us to have date-nights, so he asked me out to the movies. I was reluctant to go because I was thinking baby steps. How about a bite to eat first? He went on to say he'd had a lot of time to think, and if he had known to tell me he needed love like I told him when we first got together, things would have been different.

He put on an amazing façade. He portrayed himself as a confident, strong, secure and mature individual. When, in fact, he was broken and had low self-esteem. My mindset was different now; I didn't feel so compelled to sympathize. I felt him telling me his true feelings did explain some things. I had to also think about how he had treated me. Only a weak man hits a woman. But, I decided to go with him to the movies anyway. I needed fresh air.

He continued to talk about the changes taking place in his life. He told me he quit working at the hair salon and started working at a collection agency in West Bloomfield Hills. He told me he had changed and wanted to start dating me again so he could show me he really had changed.

I told him I was not going to take anymore verbal or physical abuse. I told him not to even try it because I'm not having it anymore. Those days are over. If he wanted me back he would have to earn my love and respect and it would take some time. When I got back from the movies, my mom was angry and said I might as well be back with him. She couldn't understand why I went to the movies with him, but if he had taken me to get something to eat it would have been okay.

I didn't like disappointing my mother and I felt as though I'd worn out my welcome. So, I decided I had to go and I'd give Klyde another chance. I moved out of my mother's house the following day and back in with him, even though I wasn't ready.

Over the last few months he had shown signs of improvement. Things did get better. He stopped the negative comments and he had a stable job. He seemed happy now. After getting hired at another collection agency in Livonia he learned the owner of the company was a young guy who also owned a mortgage company across the hall. It peaked his interest, so he made his boss a proposition.

He offered to work for free if he would teach him the mortgage business. He continued doing collections for income, but once he learned the mortgage business, the owner paid him 30% of the profit. He eventually quit the collection business and became a full time loan officer. I was glad to see a positive change in him.

Abuse or Discipline

Dear Lord,

Jade's first grade experience at Dossin Elementary was not the best. Her classmates picked on her often. They said mean things to her and tried to fight her. I was always at her school talking to someone in administration about the bullying and abuse.

One girl had pulled out some of her hair. When a parent meeting was called I learned the girl was from a single parent home and the mother was young, bitter, and didn't care. A position became available to become the president of the PTA, so I applied and got it. I wanted to change the environment of the parent/teacher relationship.

Whenever there was anything positive going on with the students or an information session, the parents would not show up. But as soon as a student got a bad grade on their report card, parents would come to the school and jump on the teacher. As the president, I was able to attend teacher workshops, meetings, and retreats. The information I learned helped me to better handle the parents.

One of the ways I drew parents to the PTA meeting was to have Klyde come in as a guest speaker to educate single mothers on credit and how they could own their own homes. We shared our testimony first, on how we were able to purchase our second home, and then gave them the tools needed to purchase their own home.

It was rewarding to be able to go before a group of women who listened to me and felt I had something to offer. Klyde was a creative mortgage loan officer and great at his job. He excelled in the mortgage business and was able to help a lot of people purchase their first homes.

Jade became the safety patrol girl at school. She did an awesome job. We only lived a few blocks from the school, but she got up extra early to make it to her post on time. Her being a safety patrol officer didn't help the jealousy the other girls had toward her. The bullying continued through her second grade year.

I could not take seeing my daughter tortured at school and no one seemed to be able to stop it. I pulled her out a few months into her second grade year. I enrolled her in Southfield Academy.

The school was a twenty minute drive from my house, but her safety and mental stability were more important than having the convenience of a school within walking distance. Her English teacher took a liking to her and took time out of the day and after school to tutor her in English. She seemed much happier in her new environment. I was glad I put my daughter's needs over mine.

Unfortunately, the damage was already done. The negativity she experienced at her old school and the things she saw at home started to manifest. She acted out and picked on her brothers. I found myself constantly disciplining her.

At her new school, she was accused of stealing $5. I didn't want to believe she did. I really trusted her when she told me she didn't take it. But not Klyde, he beat Jade vigorously until she admitted she took the money. I checked her entire body, so if she had I couldn't imagine where she could have hid it. But there it was; a $5 bill in her sock.

I don't deny she needed discipline, but not abuse. It's a thin line between being disciplined and abused. But beating a child when you're angry was different from spanking a child out of love. Physical discipline does not always solve the problem. Talking to her, sharing scriptures, and explaining right from wrong should have been the first option.

I couldn't imagine hitting Jade because it reminded me of getting hit by Klyde. I felt paralyzed whenever he whooped her. He was heavy handed and the slightest blow hurt. I know! I should have stopped him!

I didn't want her to think physical abuse was how problems were solved. It wasn't the fact he beat her and didn't explain why he was disciplining her; it was his entire outward appearance. His face curled up and a large vein popped out of his forehead. His steel biceps hit like a wrecking ball. It was painful.

I told him what he was doing was child abuse, but he assured me what he was doing was in the bible. He quoted the scripture, "spare the rod and spoil the child," from Proverbs 13:25.

I took Jade to her room and talked to her about everything. I shared scriptures with her and asked her how she could handle the situation differently next time. She told me she should have told the truth. I prayed with her and told her I loved her and so did Daddy.

The Seven Year Hump

Dear Lord,

The first seven years of marriage were supposed to be the toughest, or so I was told. If I made it to seven years, everything was supposed to be okay. Our relationship was unhealthy and extremely volatile at times. In fact, the best time was before we were married. We had a few ups, but mostly downs. I stopped telling the pastor about our marital problems because I needed to learn to depend on God and myself in order to fix my marriage.

More than half the people I knew had failed marriages within the first couple of years. I didn't want it to happen to me, but I wanted so badly to see at least a glimmer of light at the end of the tunnel.

I can't say I was ever really in love with Klyde in the way most couples fall in love, but I can say I definitely loved him unconditionally. The first time he physically abused me and had the first affair, a little bit of me chipped away. But I was deeply committed and vested in my marriage, even though things weren't as they once were.

But I was not taking it anymore. His old ways were trying to sneak back in. Before I knew it, I lashed back. Without hesitation, I cursed him out. I caught him off guard. "Oh, this is who you really are," he said. "You wouldn't be able to curse me out if it wasn't in you." What goes around definitely comes around, but this was not who I was. I was mad at myself for allowing him to get under my skin.

I finally did something that didn't meet God's standards, and Klyde was eager to tell the pastor. He told him I cursed at him and the words rolled off my tongue so easily. The Pastor had a talk with me about using profanity. Even though I felt he needed it, insulting him was mean and not the way to handle things. I told the pastor I would not allow Klyde to dictate my emotions and I would think before I spoke.

The relationship was toxic and should have been terminated, but I felt walking away was the easy way out. Standing and fighting for your family was not the norm. I wanted to stop the generational curse in my family. Too many of my family members had been divorced. Since

Klyde knew how I felt about divorce, he thought he could get away with anything. And he did! He told me if I left, if I divorced him, I couldn't get remarried, according to the bible. He told me I was damaged goods and no one will want me.

I address him by saying yes *sir*. I thought he would ask me why, but he never did. He didn't think there was anything wrong with our relationship. I told him I was unhappy and things needed to change. When we have family meetings, I sat on the floor with the children because that's the way he made me feel. Still, it appeared he was clueless there was something foul about this family.

With the confusion in our marriage, I started to think I was not fighting the battle for us, but for others. I blocked out all negativity and had faith, our relationship would get better. I knew we were going to have an awesome testimony one day. My vision was to counsel other married couples and let them know how God brought us through the war and drama. "The devil was there to steal, kill, and destroy our marriage, but I will not let the devil win!" I repeated this saying to help me through my troubles.

Chapter 8

To: Mom

(For Your Eyes Only)

To: Mom (For Your Eyes Only)

Have you ever wanted to run away and never see family again? Well, that's what I might do one day, because I feel no one cares about me. Everyone thinks I'm invisible. Everyone ignores me like I'm not even here. But, if I die while I'm out there, make my room the guest room. I'm sure everyone would love it.

Well, I might miss you. It depends on if you miss me. And don't you know when everyone says I look like you, I say I look like Daddy because he seems left out. But the person I really look like is a really ugly dog.

The only reason guys like me is because of what they see. Sometimes I think how life would be if you had only boys. Life would be so easy for you. You had to have me. I'm soooo sorry.

The boys had all good grades, but not me. You both are so happy for them. Well, with me gone dad would not have to yell as much as he does and you all can be happy all the time. Well mom, I want to make everyone happy.

Ok, well bye. Got to Go. You're calling me as always. Love you.

Dear Daughter: What Matters Most

Dear Daughter,

Yes, I have felt so alone I wanted to run away. But I realized what I would be leaving behind and what I would miss out on. Family is the most important thing in my life besides God. I love you! I want you to hear, know, and feel love.

Life would be miserable without you in it. My decision to bring a beautiful daughter to this world is God sent. I'm so glad I had you. You are so unique to me: kindhearted, artistic, creative, and intelligent.

I apologize for the pain you feel, the hurt of feeling left out or unimportant because you are important. I wouldn't know what to do without you. Don't ever leave me.

P.S. Whenever you feel sad, remember the Blueberry Prayer (The Lord is My Shepherd).

Love, Mom!

Isaiah 40:30-31

Even youth grow tired and weary,
and young men [women] stumble and fall;
but those who hope in the Lord
will renew their strength.
They will soar on wings like eagles;
they will run and not grow weary,
they will walk and not be faint.

Unconditional Love

Dear Lord,

Communication speaks volumes in a relationship and I needed my relationship to grow. In order for that to happen, I needed to talk with Sir Klyde.

On Father's Day, we were at a restaurant, he seemed uncomfortable, like he didn't want to be there. His body language and facial expressions told me he was miles away. The children sensed his uneasiness and it made them unhappy, leaving me to make excuses for his behavior. After we got home I told him he could act as if he was enjoying himself when he was with us. Children watch their parents and become imitators of them.

After the conversation, I opened the bedroom door, and to check on Jade. When headed back downstairs, I took two steps, barefooted, and slipped. I went sailing down the stairs. I didn't see anything on the floor, but somehow my feet had slipped from underneath me. I landed with my back slamming hard against the steps at the bottom. I felt like I was dreaming, like I was falling from the sky. I knew Sir was going to run down the stairs and help me, especially since I had just finished talking to him.

Throbbing pain echoed throughout my body; ringing pierced my ears as I lay with my legs twisted like a Raggedy Ann doll. I heard little footsteps running from the back of the house. It was Jade who came to my rescue. My vision was blurred, but I heard everything. I looked up into her eyes; I saw she was frightened. "Mommy, are you okay," she said. She looked up the stairs, not knowing what happened. Then she helped me up off the floor, led me to the sofa, and nursed my bruised back and sore body. She brought me a glass of water, Neosporin, and an ice pack. She showed such unconditional love through her compassion and tender spirit.

After I laid on the sofa for about an hour, Sir stood over me and said the next time I walked down the stairs I should put something on my feet and turn the light on. He also said he hoped I would learn to listen. He didn't ask how I was or if I was okay. He was insensitive and uncaring.

Every day became more evident he was not the right man for me. I wanted my marriage, but he was doing everything to destroy it. Even though I continued to stay in a relationship, my mindset started to change. But I didn't want to be defeated. I felt like we had an arrangement more than a loving marriage. If it had anything to do with business, we got along, but our personal relationship was deteriorating. Sir didn't want to admit it.

I didn't have a husband who expressed unconditional love for me, but I was glad I had a daughter who did.

My marriage had a slow leak and I kept trying to apply Fix-a-Flat. But that was a temporary fix and I needed a more lasting solution. Sooner or later it was going to deflate. I needed to strengthen myself. I needed to build myself up. I needed a positive and strong woman to mentor me, someone who could teach me how to speak up and stop getting walked on, and I found one. Mildred Gaddis, radio talk show host of "Inside Detroit." I listened to her every morning on the way to work, it was my therapy. I heard in her voice she was a strong woman. She challenged people with grace and encouraged me through her radio show and gave me fuel each day. I listened intensely as her voice elevated slightly with the strength and power of her words.

I was gradually getting stronger, my personality shifting. I did my best to find ways to build my self-esteem. Sir seemed to have made a shift as well. He wasn't treating me so badly. We started to get along better. He even took me to my first play, Tyler Perry's, "I Can Do Bad All By Myself."

The play reminded me so much of what I had gone through in our relationship. Especially the scene where she was in an upstairs bedroom and picked up the phone like she was going to hit him, but didn't because she couldn't hurt someone she loved. Why is it we can't hurt them, but they could hurt us over and over again?

The play spoke to my spirit and ministered to me. I felt an electric buzz as the play unfolded. I couldn't watch without navigating through tears; it started in my toes, raced through my legs and arms and clutched my throat. I was screaming internally, asking myself how I could have gone through so much drama.

What I didn't understand was we went to church faithfully, not as pew warmers, but active members who were involved in the ministry. We both loved the word of God and talked about how we wanted to help the church. That's why I knew behind our test and trials we were going to make it and have a powerful testimony.

Sir had experience dealing with all types of loans and brought me on board to help him answer phone calls and get the initial documents from potential clients for a mortgage loan application. Our office was located on the 2nd floor office of a beautiful building in Bloomfield Hills.

Sir was charismatic and knew exactly what to say to clients. When I spoke to clients it was all business, but he taught me how be personable and make small talk before talking business.

Sir was an expert storyteller. Everyone loved him around the office. He was funny, charming, entertaining and had a big personality. And of course everyone thought he was the perfect husband.

After a few months working as Sir Klyde's assistant, Rick, the processing manager, came in to speak to us. Martin wanted to see our business grow, so he asked if I would be interested in learning how to process loan applications. I said, "Sure."

I learned the mortgage business quickly, but I became disappointed when I heard my husband say he didn't believe I could it. I was very frustrated with him, not because I spent eight hours in the office and wasn't getting paid for it, but because he wasn't closing any more loans.

I was not asking for instant results, but several months passed and he was closing fewer and fewer. Why, was my question? I was doing the paperwork, he was out of the office meeting clients and looking for new business all the time. At least that's what he told me.

I was usually in the office before Klyde. This particular morning, I called him on his cell phone and said, "Good morning, how are you? I miss you." But he did not recognize my voice. "Who's calling," he said. I took offense. After ten years, he didn't know his own wife's voice.

I imagined I would be the most important person in his life. "Who else would be calling you at 6:30 a.m. and telling you I miss you," I said. All of a sudden, "it's static in the phone, I can't hear you," he said. "I'll see you in a minute." When he got to work, it was business as usually. No discussion about how he didn't recognize my voice, until I confronted him about it.

What bothered me about Sir was he spoke highly of other women. Marge, who had a master's degree in special education, came up in conversations all the time. He spoke to her on the phone often, he even invited her over. Every time I talked about furthering my education he discouraged me and told me it wasn't a good time. "You want to move, right," he asked. "So we need to make more money in order to do that. If you go to school, it will take longer to save money."

He loved successful women. Whenever they had some kind of issue with their business, house, or whatever the case may be, he swooped down like a knight in shining armor and saved them. He was a hero and the master at finding a damsel in distress. Although, he told me he was frustrated single women called him to do odds and ends for them, like they didn't have anyone else to call.

One of his friends was a slightly older woman, Ms. Grey who owned her own mortgage company. We'd met and spoke on many occasions. Since she was older with two teenaged daughters. She became part of our lives. Sir spent a lot of time helping her with her business and things around her house. She started coming to our church. I was a private person and no one knew much about me outside of church. But I needed advice on how to best raise my children.

I thought she'd be a great person who could share wisdom with me. She told me to get prepared because one day my little girl will try to dominate me and take on a wife role and act like she knew more about my husband than I did.

Interesting information I thought, but I couldn't see that happening. Sir spent most of his time learning about the new mortgage business. To the world he was the best husband and father one could possibly have. He was convincing. He told a story in a way you'd believe you were there. I think he missed his calling.

He told me he needed help covering the bills and wanted me to ask my dad for a loan, but I was tired of asking my dad to borrow money. My dad always asked if it was for an investment or for bills. He didn't mind investing in a business, but it was never for investments always to pay our monthly bills. This was another reason my dad didn't like him. He couldn't take care of his family.

Whenever possible, I'd work with my brother to make extra money. I'd help with painting, home improvement tasks, or cleaning buildings. Jade helped by selling candy at church and school.

Intimidated by a Child

Dear Lord,

Jade was in the 5th grade, her height had superseded mine. Her strong personality towered over me. I felt intimidated by her outspokenness and resilient will. I found myself always mad at her. If she did the slightest thing wrong, all my attention went toward the negative event.

I wouldn't whoop her when I was mad, but I could stay mad at her all day. I even yelled sometimes. She started to become very aggressive. I wondered if it had anything to do with seeing me get abused all her life.

She seemed angry all the time and was constantly getting into trouble at school. Her brothers thought she was mean. They called her The Punisher because she choked, slapped, and slammed them around. She antagonized them until they got mad. It was okay to stand up for herself, but not okay to taunt or incite others.

She was not always like this. She used to be happy all the time. She jumped around smiling, laughing, and playing by herself. She was so content and pleased. I guess after years of disappointments, things started to change.

My frustration came from more than intimidation I was also jealous of her because of the jolly spirit I sometimes saw and how she was able to express herself to me. I couldn't understand how she was so happy at times, especially when I was sad and miserable.

I remembered saying what's there to be so happy about and telling her she needed to grow up. Why do we find fault in what other people are doing? I had issues too and wasn't showing her the attention she needed.

I wanted to cuddle her sometimes, but I didn't know how, I felt detached. I would look at her, trying to figure out what was holding me back. I thought if I told her to scoot down on the couch or maybe if I sat on a stack of blankets I'd feel taller than her. But it felt awkward. Even talking to her was challenging. I found myself arguing with her and always pointing out what she did wrong.

The bible says to train a child in the way they should go, but she and I couldn't see eye to eye. She got sassy with me and didn't listen. I wanted to teach her things, but I didn't know how to reach her. How did I show her love when I felt like I was competing with her? My own daughter!

Even though I had these feelings, I still tried to encourage her dad to start a father daughter day with Jade so she could feel special. I thought it was important for a daughter to get fatherly love so she would never let men run over her. Jade would come to me and say, "Dad is going to buy a new car, he told me first and I thought you should know."

I should have been prepared for the misplaced behavior because Ms. Grey once told me there was going to come a time when my daughter would feel superior to me. She told me I had to watch and be careful because it could destroy our relationship, but not to give in; to be strong and reach out to her because she will need my love.

My sister, Denise, told me Jade was reaching out for my love and attention, but it didn't register at the time. I thought it was more important for her to spend time with her dad because I was always there. But being there and being present are two different things.

"Lord, please take the spirit of resentment, anger and negatively away from me. I want to love my little girl unconditionally. I need for us to have a mother/daughter relationship that mother's dream of. I want to thank you in advance, Lord, for changing my mindset, changing my circumstances, and showing me how to love my daughter."

Bully or Be Bullied

Dear Lord,

One evening, Jade came into my bedroom, looked at me, and hesitated as if she was about to say something. She then turned to walk away, but turned back and said, "Mom, why are you letting people walk over you? You have to speak up. Even the boys are treating you badly." She felt I let her brothers get away with too much. She said I raised her right, to be an independent and strong woman of God.

Whenever the boys didn't do what she wanted, she hit them. She didn't want them walking all over her. She was the oldest and she was going to have respect. She'd even get on them like she was the mother. If I told her to tell the boys something, she translated it into what she thought I meant.

I didn't get what she was saying to me. Everything seemed normal. I thought I was raising the boys the same way I raised her. She told me I didn't speak up enough, I let her down and she thought I was weak. But I felt like I was strong to have endured such heartache and pain over so

177

many years.

I wanted to speak up, but I had been taught it takes two to argue and maybe it would stop if I stayed quiet. I didn't want my daughter to think abuse was normal in a marriage. My thinking might not have made sense to her, but it made sense to me.

Change is Coming

Dear Lord,

Sir accused me of caring more about the church than him. My heavenly father meant the world to me. I was willing to sacrifice my life for what I believed in. Without my heavenly father in my life, I was nothing. God's grace brought me through some very rough times.

What I came to realize was the only good thing from my marriage was our three beautiful children...for the most part. I felt our relationship was built on a foundation of quicksand, mixed with lies, deceit, and betrayal.

I often wondered whether the physical abuse would stop completely or was he taking a break. Everything seemed better, but the rage would always seep through. I felt if I didn't stand up for something I would continue to take anything. I like the scripture, "Seek ye first the kingdom of God and all his righteousness and all things will come to us" (Matthew 6:33). I pray for the Lord to use me to his honor and glory, and I will serve him every day of my life.

During the altar call, the pastor invited people to come forward who were seeking deliverance and to hear a word from the Lord. I went up. I must gain courage and peace. As I walked back to my seat, Sister Strong reached for my arm and pulled me toward her. With tears in my eyes, I leaned down to her and with a soft voice she told me, "It's time for you to move up from the back. Step out of the shadows, speak up and let your light shine. Let God use you."

I hugged her and took my seat. My spirit shook. I thought, "but I didn't mind being in the background." I was comfortable there. I felt this was God speaking through her because we had never had a conversation. She didn't know me. I wanted to be obedient to what God was saying, so I asked the Lord to use me. My fears started drifting away. I was no longer comfortable working for Sir. I started noticing uneasiness with the way my life was going.

I kept repeating in my mind what Sister Strong said. I didn't mind working in the background and not being noticed. Sir was great at public speaking. He loved being up front and the center of attention, but maybe God wanted me to change.

I always stood by Sir Klyde's side when he spoke in front of the church. I would say a few

180

words, but I was quiet and shy. I needed to figure out how to change and be the person I felt I was being guided to be. It was difficult to have a conversation with someone and whenever someone looked at me I would turn away and look down. Pastor would say, "If you want friends, you need to make yourself friendly." I always felt he could read my mind and tell me exactly what I needed to help me.

By becoming an usher, I had to talk to people. I would stand along the side of the wall and scan the audience. I noticed people watching me. It was a natural reaction for people to look, so I thought nothing of it. I made an effort to talk to people. Sister Runner was over the sisterhood committee. She befriended me and took me under her wing.

She included me in her life, invited me to family functions, and had me speaking at women's conferences and church events on finance, budgeting, and saving money. I was nervous. I also spoke in front of my church and in small settings. It was a wonderful experience. I wondered if she knew the impact she had on my life. She helped me build confidence.

My Dad's Heart Attack

Dear Lord,

    I told my dad he didn't have to watch Ja'von anymore because he was accepted in an all-day kindergarten program. The following day, I was getting ready for church when I received a call from my brother saying Dorothy, my dad's girlfriend, said my dad was in the hospital. He plopped down in the living room chair, but when she woke up he wasn't breathing, so she called an ambulance. I heard what he said, but my thoughts were jumbled and I thought it wasn't serious. He may be in a coma, but he's going to wake up.

    When I arrived at Pontiac Hospital, I briskly walked through the emergency room trying to remain calm. I went to his bedside and he was lying peacefully. His eyes were closed, and it looked like he almost had a smirk on his face. I was waiting on him to open his eyes. What my brother told me didn't register. They tried to resuscitate him in the ambulance, but they pronounced him dead on arrival. My brother walked to me and said, "He's in a better place now."

I didn't know what else to do but grab and hold him. Tears rolled down my face. My father was only sixty-five. It was too soon. I was not ready for him to die yet. I needed him. He was a person I could sit with and feel comfort, never any drama, only peace and a smile. All I could think about was how sad he looked when I told him Ja'von got accepted to an all-day kindergarten program. It was as if his assignment was over, and it was time for him to go.

When I told Sir what happened, he said, "I'm sorry to hear that. He was a cool dude." No hug, no outward emotion. I needed my husband. My family embraced each other with a hug in good times and bad. Sir told me I loved my family more than I loved him. He was jealous and kept me away from them as much as possible. I missed family reunions because of him. My dad even offered to pay for Jade and me to go to the family reunion, but I turned him down.

What was I thinking? It was a chance for me to escape this life for a couple of days, but I felt crippled and trapped. Now he was gone and couldn't be replaced.

I was mad and flustered. He had no compassion. I was hurting and felt alone. I thought back to how my dad never liked Sir and wanted me to leave him. He even told me he would take care of the children and me, but I never took him up on his offer.

I took my dad's death hard. My purpose in life vanished and without him, life terrified me. He was built on solid ground and without him I felt like I was going to fall apart. He was a man of little words, but his presence shouted strength. Family and friends brought us food, but the stress caused me to lose a ton of weight. I lay awake at night wondering what life was going to be like without my dad.

I didn't realize how close Jade had gotten to him. I was so caught up in my own feelings I lost sight of everything around me. I found a note Jade had written about how she missed her grandfather and how she was hurting so badly. I went to hug her and told her I was sorry I didn't realize how her grandfather's death affected her. I was caught up in my own sorrow. She went on to share stories about the times they shared together. The scary movies I wouldn't let her watch he did, how he loved to cook and take her to the park.

I Tried to Take My Own Life

Dear Lord,

The day came to bury my father. We decided on a homegoing service instead of a funeral because we wanted to celebrate his life for what it was, laughter and warmth. He was the one who brought everyone together for cookouts.

One would be held in Detroit and the other in Jackson, Mississippi where his plot was for extended family. Everyone decided to wear black because it was the color most of us had. My funeral attire had grown in importance from something that should have been simple, to the most important thing. I wanted to be in unison with my sisters and brothers. I looked in my closet, and nothing seemed right. I wondered where I was going to get the money to buy a new outfit.

I discussed with Sir all in my family were wearing black, and I had nothing to wear. To him, it was a simple fix; we didn't have the money, so wear whatever I had. "If I'd borrowed $5,000 from your daddy we wouldn't have had to pay it back, and I would have had the money to buy an outfit," told me. We always seem to have money when he wanted to buy music, electronic devices or perm for his hair.

All of this was overwhelming. He was insensitive. I was mourning the passing of my dad and one thing that would have brought me sense of comfort was to wear black at the funeral. I was not going to wear grey, blue or any other color.

I was too embarrassed to tell my family I couldn't afford to buy an outfit. I pondered for a while then I remembered I had a credit card. I drove to Lord and Taylor at Fairlane Mall and bought the perfect suit. When Klyde came home, I told him I found a way to buy an outfit. He yelled at me and said, "Didn't I tell you not to buy anything." He stormed out of the house.

Dark thoughts ran through my mind. I started hearing, it's okay. Your kids are older now. They can take care of themselves. Your daddy's gone, he can't protect you now. It's going to be okay. Do it. No one will miss you. I anxiously walked back and forth in my bedroom, feeling restless, incomplete, disrespected and not loved.

I went into the bathroom, undressed, stared at myself in the mirror and didn't recognize the person there. I opened the medicine cabinet and took out the bottle of a large bottle of Advil. Got into the shower and slowly put pills in my mouth. Then I stuck my head under the showerhead, opened my mouth and swallowed. Then I put more and more, shoving handfuls of pills down my throat. One after another until the bottle was empty. My stomach was full. I leaned against the shower wall, stumbled out of the shower, and bumped into the wall. I got a cold shiver. I felt light headed.

By this time, Sir had come home, opened the bedroom door with a bag in his hand. With blurred vision and slurred words I said, "You could buy an S-curl hair texturizer for your hair but I couldn't buy an outfit for my dead father's funeral." That's why I took a bottle of pills. I was like a drunken person, stumbling and slurring my words. He said, "Why would you do this to me?" It's always about him. While I struggled to put my clothes on, he combed perm through his hair. I ask when he would be ready to go to my dad's funeral. "I'm not going," he said. He wasn't going! "Can you at least drop me off, I can't see."

"That's not my problem," he said.

I put all three the children in the car. By the time, I got in my vision hard worsened. I started to drift in and out of consciousness. I thought about having Jade drive, but she wasn't old enough. As I drove towards the freeway I started nodding a bit and tried to shake it off. I decided the freeway wasn't a good option, so I took a side street. I wasn't sure which streets I took or how long it took me to get there. But I looked up and noticed I was at the funeral home.

I asked Jade to get my sisters. After they lifted my head off the steering wheel, they asked how I got there. I said, "I drove." My sister and brother helped me inside. I couldn't sit up without their support, so I sat on the pew between their arms. I felt sick to the stomach. So they helped me to the bathroom. I hovered over the toilet. Nothing came out. Natalie from church came in to see about me. My sister would not let her in, but I said, it's okay. Natalie prayed for me and eventually I got up. She helped sit me into a chair outside the bathroom.

My pastor came along shortly; my sister told him I was asleep. I was sitting straight up in a chair with my eyes closed. I felt paralyzed. My insides twisted like someone was playing tug of war. He held my hand, talked to me and prayed for me. I wanted him to know I knew he was there. So with all my strength I squeezed his hand. I heard him say, "She knows I'm here."

My sister came back to take me into the service. However, I physically couldn't, so we sat in the hall where it was standing room only; I laid on the bench across both sisters.

After the funeral was over everyone was going to my mom's house. I knew something was terribly wrong, I felt my spirits lifting from my soul. I was lifeless as though being lifted away. Darkness was all around me with a glimmer of light.

The pain in my stomach was so severe I wanted it to stop. I asked Sir to take me to the hospital, reluctant, but he did. He complained all the way how could I do this to him. I was the one in pain. The nurses asked me questions tested me and strapped me to the bed. I was helpless, bonded and shackled. Not knowing whether I was going to live or die. I took so many pills, but I told myself I only took a hand full. The test said otherwise.

The doctor gave me black charcoal to absorb the Advil and I threw-up the medicine. Moving fast on the inside was emptiness like a cold shiver mixed with an upset stomach. I wanted to slow down. I wanted the pain to stop. I prayed to God and made a promise if he took away the pain I would never try to take my own life again

The following day my brother rented a tour bus to drive the whole family to Jackson,

Mississippi for a homegoing service. I wanted the doctor to release me from the hospital. They wanted me admitted in the psych ward for observation for a week but I convinced the doctors it was a mistake, but they still ordered me to see a psychiatrist on an outpatient basis. That was the only way the doctor would let me go. I was released right before the bus left, but I didn't feel up to riding with everyone so I asked Sir to drive me. He told me no, ride the bus with my family.

My stomach and head still felt faint and weak, I was unable to look after the children. I was sad and disappointed, trying to hide my true feelings from my family. After I got to Mississippi the next morning, I was on my way to my mother's room when Sir popped his head out one of the rooms. I had a look of disguise on my face, he thought I should have been happy to see him, but I was mad and disappointed. He made the children and me take an uncomfortable twenty-one hour bus ride south and he came down anyway. I couldn't see past his selfishness.

His *surprise* backfired. He told me he made it to Mississippi in seventeen hours. I knew it was all a show. Since my response was not as he thought it should be, he told everyone I was insensitive. Back home in Detroit, he told Pastor

Wyndham and everyone he came in contact with that he drove eighteen hours straight down to Jackson, Mississippi, got a hotel room and surprised me by getting there before I did. What occurred to me was he found fault in everything I did, he wanted people to feel sorry for him, and they did.

He painted the picture he wanted them to see, but they didn't know there was another picture on the other side. After we buried my dad, we needed to handle his estate. My dad was an awesome businessman; he never lacked money. He claimed he had a last will and testament drawn up. However, no one knew where it was. I hired an attorney to handle the logistics.

Whenever I needed to borrow money, he would go out to the shed in the backyard and come back with thousands of dollars. He'd say, "I won't not charge you interest, but I want it back the same way I gave it to you." He had money not only in the shed but also in the walls, in the ceiling and the entire house including the bank. No one knew where he hid the will so we started to think he never had one. After a few months, the estate was handled through the probate court.

Before he passed, I spoke to him about moving closer to him. He never felt truly comfortable with my marriage, but he thought it got better. With my inheritance, we were able to move out of Detroit to Rochester Hills. Greatschools.org rated Rochester Community School District with a score of 10 out of 10.

Since we were living in the suburbs, I thought things would be better. Sir Klyde's behavior was strange. He would stand on the porch gazing down street with a blank stare, unaware I stood in the doorway watching him. It was a lonely helpless look. I was glad we moved, but I wished the verbal abuse stopped. He was a ticking time bomb; you never knew when he'd go off. I slept at night with a knife under the mattress. I didn't want to use it, but I would if I had too.

I was tired of my children watching me verbally abused. Jade thought I was weak and didn't stand up for myself, but it takes two to argue. Before he came home, I made sure everything was clean and in order. He always complained about something. The children scattered whenever they heard his car pull up. They'd run and get in the bed and act like they were asleep. The children were scared of Sir, but I made them talk to him and give him a hug. I told Sir he needed to show love to the children and stop treating them badly. They were scared to talk to him. But I found out later, he'd whoop them, and tell them *I* was the one not letting them do things. We needed to make choices toward being a loving and devoted couple (peacemaker) instead of destroying it.

Since the children, saw him as an evil troll, he wanted them to like him. So he asked me to be the bad person, but why should I have to be mean? He needed to be more loving.

Fire in the House

Dear Lord,

Most Sundays Sir and I drove separate to the church because once a month I taught Sunday school class and worked in the nursery. Usually after church service we stayed and socialized, but Jade's homework was due Monday, so after church, we went directly home.

On the drive home heat radiated through the windows from the afternoon sun. I drove to the sound of birds chirping when two deer darted out of the grassy pasture and ran across the road.

We passed by children laughing and playing as we drove into the driveway. The children changed out of their church clothes. I went into the office and logged onto the computer for Jade. I called Jade in and helped her get started on her homework. We were all hungry so I went into the kitchen and pulled out the chicken I seasoned the night before from the refrigerator. I put grease in a pan and turned on stove.

I went back into the office for about a minute

or two before I smelled something odd entering the room. I ran to the kitchen. The stove was in flames and smoke went from the skillet to the ceiling. So many thoughts went through my mind about what to do and what not to do. I didn't want to put water on flames; I thought it might spread or worse, jump on me. I yelled for the children to go outside

My first call was to Sir since he wasn't far away. The second call was to the police who dispatched the fire department. When Sir got home he and a neighbor went to the back of the house with a water hose. Neighbors came out of their homes, stood in the street watching the smoke pour from the house. A fireman asked me who I called first. I said my husband. He said they should always be the first ones called.

The house had so much smoke damage our State Farm insurance policy paid for us to stay in an apartment until the house was repaired. From insurance money, we were able to transform our house to a state of the art contemporary home. We added granite countertops, stainless steel appliances and two-toned hardwood flooring throughout.

While remodeling, Sir rode his motorcycle every chance he got. I didn't blame him because riding was like skimming a wave of peace. It was relaxing but also released an instant thrill. Nothing could compare. I needed to be in the driver's seat; the back didn't do it.

Thursdays were "Bike Night" at Royal Oak off Main Street. I was already in bed when Sir came home acting strangely. He sat me up on the edge of the bed grabbed my hands and said, "Pray for me." I said, "Sure, but what's wrong?" He said, "Nothing, I felt like the devil is trying to attack my mind."

I said, "Is it a woman, do you feel like you're getting weak and might sleep with someone else." He said, "No, nothing like that. I need you to pray for my mind." I said, "Okay." I prayed for him.

My sister Soni visited to celebrate Labor Day with us at Borden Park in Rochester Hills. She hadn't been there long before Sir came home from riding his motorcycle. He needed to talk to me before we left so we went into the bedroom.

He was in heat and needed a fix. I told him I couldn't; my sister and the children were waiting outside the room for me. Then I thought back on the week before about needing me to pray for him. Even though he said it wasn't temptation, I didn't want him to cheat so I gave him a fix and told him I'll give him more later. He gave me a pleasing smile and said, "Okay."

We both went our separate ways. The children, my sister, and I went to the Borden Festival and Fireworks show. I arrived home after 10:00 p.m., tired, put the children to bed and I went to sleep. When Sir came home, he woke me up and said, "Do you remember how understanding I was when, you told me, you slept with your friend Nick?"

The first thought was, what the heck, why was he bringing up the past and he remembered his name. I told him it was over ten years ago after he slept with Cookie from the hair salon. Kneeling down with his head on my lap, he said, "I made a mistake, I had sex with someone," he said.

Even though I felt he warned me the week prior I smacked him across his face. Then he told me he had a sex problem and didn't want me to know because I wouldn't have married him if I knew.

He cheated me out of the opportunity to make the decision whether to marry him, and I was angry. But he looked like a little puppy making me feel sorry for him when he said he had a sex addiction. I viewed it as a drug addiction and told him he needed help from the pastor, a counselor, somebody.

This explained a lot about my sexually transmitted diseases. I knew the old saying if he accuses me then he is the one cheating. Before any issues crept up in my body, I went to see my cousin AJ, an internal medicine doctor in Southfield, Michigan. I told Sir he had to get checked out too.

"What do I tell him the reason I need to get tested for STD?" Sir said. I said, "The truth."

Everything in me was saying this was it. What was a doormat used for? To wipe your feet and keep moving, it lays there and does nothing, just like me. I leave; I come back waiting to be stepped on again and again.

Each day I grew more bitter toward him. I wanted answers but his reasoning didn't make sense. I wanted to know how long the affair had been going on. Was it as he said, he stopped at a hotel to use the rest room but ended up outside in a red Jeep having sex with a church member.

I looked through the mobile phone bill and found phone conversations between him and the woman from the early morning hours and through the day. The records went back at least a year.

198

Whenever I tried to talk to him in the morning, he said he was going back to sleep. Right under my nose and didn't see it. I thought to myself Jesus died for the church, so I didn't have to. I began my own investigation and found her first and last name and where she worked.

I documented everything that happened in my journal, her address and phone number, even her relative's names. She was married; I had met both her and her husband when they came into the office for a mortgage loan a few month prior.

I felt dumb. How many people has he slept with at church, are they laughing at me. This is what I thought. How could I be so naive?

I cooked breakfast, lunch and dinner for this man. I warmed his plate and serve him as a king. His co-workers would say *I wish I had a wife like her*. I struggled every day. I sacrificed my life for him. I felt obligated to the church and wondered if the other couples would see us as failures.

I felt this way because Sir was always in front of the church doing financial seminars, or taking photos at services and events. He served as a pastor's armor bearer. He went out of town and served the pastor well. Only if he knew how Sir was tearing his family apart. I asked him to confide in the pastor and seek advice.

I went to church faithfully but was dying on the inside. I was one of the leaders in Sunday school for three, four and five years old and worked in the nursery. I loved church, I loved working with children.

The church thought we were the perfect couple. If we broke up, this would disappoint the church and give a pass for others to divorce. This was a heavy burden to carry, but I couldn't stand to see someone fall based on my account. But everything inside me was screaming I needed a release of peace. I was mentally done with the relationship. But trapped in a vicious cycle of a battered woman syndrome.

My best friend Mindy didn't know what was going on. I kept it to myself. Sir drilled me on how she didn't tell me anything about her husband Marlie so I shouldn't tell her anything. I needed to get all the frustration out somehow. So I called the other woman at work. I asked a couple of questions anonymously gathering information to later confront her. I didn't understand why I was going through so much. Over the years, I'd taken physical and mental abuse. I wanted her to feel my pain.

While at work at Paramount Bank I planned to leave and talk to this woman. I sat at my desk and

200

prayed for God to show me the way.

As I worked, I prayed and suddenly I heard an audible voice talking to me. Telling me to be still, to stay, don't rush into anything, stay! Confused, I looked around I said, "wait." When I stopped praying, the voice stopped.

I thought this isn't real. I wanted to hear more. I started praying again, and I heard the words clearly, "Be still, stay, wait on the Lord."

It was a voice I never heard before. It startled me. I've heard of people talking about God speaking to them. But I wondered if it was God or Satan trying to get me to stay. I didn't know. And if it were God, I didn't know if he meant: don't go see her or stay in the marriage. I love the Lord unconditionally, and willing to do anything he told me to do, even if I didn't agree and this was one of those times. So I stayed and waited until I heard from God again.

"Forgiveness is not a feeling - it's a decision we make because we want to do what's right before God. It's a quality decision that won't be easy and it may take time to get through the process, depending on the severity of the offense." Joyce Meyer

Chapter 9
DEFENSE OR OFFENSE

Dear Lord,

Jade told a lie. She said she was not talking on the phone. It was around 9:00 p.m. She didn't realize we heard her talking. Sir crossed to the white sofa, snatched her up and said, "Don't ever lie to me again," and slammed her onto the sofa. He picked her up again and threw her again the wall. He started shaking her, and throwing her down.

With me there, frozen, I had a flashback. He hadn't physically hit me in a couple years. But, he never stopped mentally abusing me. I couldn't believe what I was seeing. The abuse had transferred from me to Jade. And it dawned on me later that some part of me was glad it wasn't me.

She pleaded. Please stop, Please stop, that's enough. This is abuse! I yelled, STOP! STOP!

Please stop! Enough! That's enough. She yelled out again. "I'm going to call the police!" Oh, why did she say that?

As he picked her up and slammed her, he said, "I dare you! Call the police." But I guess he got scared she might, so he unplugged the cable, and the phone from the wall. Picked her up, slung her around like a rag doll. Picked her up again and she was airborne, landing across the room.

He didn't stop until he was ready. He huffed and puffed, out of breath as though he ran a marathon. With two balled up fists, he said, "Now I guess you won't lie to me again. Get up and go to bed." She was shaking and crying all the way to her bedroom.

I went to her. "You should not have lied, and we heard you on the phone." She looked at me with wounded eyes. Then I told her she didn't deserve to be treated that way and I was sorry. She cried.

Sir always told me we had to be on one chord and the children could never know we disagreed with the punishment. At the time, I didn't know I was abusing her too. She told me I stood by, watched and did nothing.

In my mind I did speak up, I tried to make it less painful. I thought I protected her. But her behavior towards her brothers was brutal at times, and I felt

204

punishment was warrant, but not to the extreme she received. She went to school mad and upset: acted out, got into fights, and argued with teachers. She seemed to not listen to me, but whatever her dad told her to do, she'd do.

Her school suggested counseling at Rochester Adams Youth Center. After going a few times, they suggested family counseling was needed. Her behavior was random and misplaced, but they didn't know how to reach her.

She didn't have material things--toys, phone, or anything we could take away as a punishment for her behavior, so Sir decided she'd sleep in the basement. I helped her move a few of her things. The basement was unfinished with no furniture. The only things were boxes and a wooden door. I tried to make the door a comfortable bed by padding it with a lot of blankets. I wanted to believe Sir was trying to help her change and not be so mean to her brothers, but I felt bad she had to sleep in the basement, on a door. I didn't understand his thinking, but I supported him.

I tried to come up with other punishments. He suggested taking church functions away such as the praise team as punishment, but I disagreed. He compromised by only having her miss one practice and taking her jeans. He thought by him keeping her jeans she would act more like a lady and would stop her from hitting her brothers. Taking away her jeans was right up my alley because I felt I was losing control. We had already talked about how her body was starting to develop. We didn't want attention drawn to her shapely figure. So, he sent her to school in dresses and skirts.

Sir took all her jeans and put them in his closet. He missed a few so I went into her room and took the rest and hid them under my bed and in my closet. In my eyes, she was still my little girl and needed protection from the teenage boys. My baby was growing up and I wasn't ready for it.

Looking back, this was cruel punishment. Why the basement? Why not any other reprimand? We talked about punishment together and I agreed to most. However, I didn't know he made her believe it was all *my* idea. I understood why she couldn't stand me.

I told Sir he was the first impression of a man his daughter would encounter. She was watching and taking notes. But I didn't understand how important my role was. I was the first impression of how a woman should be. My reaction, what I allowed, played a huge part in what she would allow and how she would treat others.

Isaiah 41:10

Fear not, for I am with you;
be not dismayed,
for I am your God;
I will strengthen you,
I will help you,
I will uphold you with my
righteous right hand.

Jade tries to commit suicide

Dear Lord,

During one of our mother daughter talks, I shared with Jade what happened to me after her grandfather died. I wanted her to know, to respect, and love herself more than she loved a man and not to do anything to harm herself over a man.

Months later Jade came home sluggish, and complained she didn't feel good. I asked her what her symptoms were. She told me she was weak her whole body was cold and numb. I took her temperature, tried to comfort her.

She didn't want anything to eat. I asked her what happened, was everything okay. She told me she had a headache all day today. So she kept taking pills her friends gave her, plus ones from home to make the pain go away. I helped her to bed.

I sat next to her on the mattress, her breathing was shallow, body limp and temperature was cold to the touch. I covered her body with blankets. I looked into her distant eyes when she said, "I don't want to go to sleep; I might die and not wake up."

I told Sir I thought something was seriously wrong with Jade, and I was taking her to the emergency room. On the way out the door, he told her to hurry back so she could clean the kitchen. Not 'I hope you feel better.' Jade never forgot his words.

I took take her to Crittenton Hospital near downtown Rochester. They tested her for all sorts of things. The doctor concluded she overdosed on contraband. She tried to convince me it was an accident.

I couldn't stop thinking how I told her about trying to commit suicide myself and thought if I hadn't told her, maybe she would have never tried it. I looked up facilities to help Jade deal with her negative emotions. Sir resisted, he did not want me to take her. A couple of evenings later I snuck out and took her to Havenwick in Pontiac; Jade was so angry with me for taking her, but I needed her to stay around. I was concerned and wanted to help her.

I admitted her, but right before I finished the paperwork, Sir showed up. He walked in behind me with a fierce look on his face; I was completely terrified. I didn't understand how he found me when I was driving a different car. I was scared because I didn't know what he was going to do to me. I stalled, but I couldn't stay in the bathroom forever.

I called my friend Mercedes and talked to her for least forty minutes and told her what was going on. Not knowing when I walked out of the women's bathroom, he would be standing, blocking the entrance.

He questioned me who I was talking to. I ask him to step aside. He said no, he wanted to talk to me. "Who were you talking to," he said.

"What does it matter," I said, and tried to walked around him.

He said, "Why did you do this? I told you I didn't want her here." She was going through a lot and having a hard time coping. I explained he had not protected her. I told him we should walk outside, I had to leave. He went and stood by a big monster truck. I thought he might run me over. So I jumped into the car and pulled off.

Jade stayed at Havenwick for two weeks. Visiting hours were limited, and phone calls were few. I made up excuses to my family where Jade was. I didn't want anyone to know what she or I were going through.

After her release, we went to family

counseling, not Sir, only the children and me. The counselor would never tell me what they spoke about, but she repeated I needed to listen to my daughter and get out of the situation I was in. I wanted more information. I didn't want to break up the family structure.

We went to counseling for months until the counselor would not accept my calls anymore. If I was not going to change the situation, she did not want to be a part of the breakdown.

I took Jade to the neighborhood physiologist. I didn't realize how unhappy she was. The psychologist pleaded with me to save my daughter. She encouraged me to get out of the situation I was in without revealing the conversation she and Jade had.

I didn't want to leave home. It was my decision, not my daughter's. Right? At that moment, I had no biblical reason to leave. Or did I?

I knew my family was dysfunctional but wasn't it better to have a two parent household? Better to have a piece of man than no man at all, it's better for the children if he's in the home.

I didn't want to accept this marriage was going to fail. In my mind, it was going to work.

All I had to do was convince myself everything was okay. I made excuses why things were so bad. I blamed myself. I started to see I couldn't keep the blinders on. I had to change. Staying in an abusive marriage was not healthy not only for me, but the children, too.

Whale Done

Dear Diary,

 I didn't get it. I didn't get the notes and letters Jade slid under my bedroom door were a way of her tapping me on the shoulder. To say, "Mom, here I am, look at me, I need you."

 She would ask to talk to me. I would say, sure, but at the same time, I would be cooking, cleaning, ironing, and many other things. She would say, Mom, you are not paying attention to me. My response was, "Yes, I am." She'd say I paid attention to the boys.

 As a mom, a lot of responsibility followed the title such as, homemaker, maid, family mascot/boss, referee, nurse, therapist, personal chef, tutor/teacher, chauffeur, administrative assistant – the list goes on and on. Not to mention I did all of this while working a full time job and attending school functions. Plus taking care of her younger brothers.

 I wanted my children to have as close to a healthy happy home as possible. I blamed myself for allowing the abuse to go on so long and made excuses for Sir Klyde's behavior. I told myself he didn't know how to love his family.

Since he didn't know how to love us, I felt I was married, but living single. All my responsibilities were overwhelming. To outsiders, it looked as though I was handling things well. But, internally, at times I was a wreck. Whenever she slid a note under my door or left one where only I could see, it reminded me she was missing something. It never dawned on me the thing she was missing was me.

Jade was in eighth grade when I prayed for the Lord to show me how to reach her; one day I listened. I heard a well-known speaker, Kenneth Blanchard, explain the most efficient way to get the best performance from people was to accentuate the positive qualities in their nature by redirecting the negative.

He spoke about a book called "Whale Done: the power of positive relationships." He wrote the book with top SeaWorld trainers. I was in desperate need to change the negative behavior she displayed on a regular basis. It only provoked negative attention.

I bought the audio version of the book determined to learn another way. I learned to find positive things to compliment her on and reward positive behavior. I overlooked most of the negative things she did. It showed me the way I was doing things was not the best way to handle her. I wanted to be a better mother and show her the love she was seeking. I knew she was unaware of the measures I took to become a better mother.

Learning new techniques changed the way I responded to her and changed her behavior. It was difficult at first not to say or point out the negative. Especially when the principal would call and say your daughter got into another altercation and choked a girl during lunch.

It was also hard to stop everything I was doing to give her undivided attention. But, I knew stopping to talk with her meant a lot. So, I tried to do that until I didn't have to try anymore.

With prayer and darkness far behind me, my vision and mental state were clear. We could start to grow and develop a loving relationship.

Thank you, Lord, for answering my prayers!

Peace

Dear Lord,

One thing I could truly say about my natural father was he was a peacemaker. "Don't worry about the dumb stuff; you need peace of mind," he would say all the time. I searched the scriptures after he got sick, and saw it wasn't some random saying; it was biblical.

In order for our relationship to work, we needed God and peace. Searching the scriptures, I found discovered the word *peace* was in almost every book of the Bible. In the Old Testament, peace was a sought after commodity. God is the God of Peace. When peace was removed, all hell broke loose. I told Sir he and I had the opportunity to be peacemakers if we seek peace. Peace will dwell in us. "When a man's ways please the Lord, he makes even his enemies to be at peace with him." Proverbs 16:7

I didn't understand what I was waiting for anymore. This man was going to be what he always had been. I starting to think I misinterpreted what God told me to do. What did he mean when he told me to wait and be still?

I wanted to be married and I wanted my children to experience Godly marriage. Parents who love and adored each other; who kept the peace and brought peace to his or her family. I prayed he'd seek and pursue the peace of mind my daddy also spoke about.

I'd tried to fix the problem but I couldn't. I had to turn it over to God. I prayed the prayer, ...Father God, May the peace that passes all understanding rest upon us. Guide our hearts, minds, body and souls to be fully under you. I release and surrender. In Jesus's name, amen! Philippians 4:7

Love and Affection

Dear Lord,

My life felt like I was traveling through time as a walking stick, clueless of my surrounding. I had gradually become codependent on Sir. I held onto his every word as gold. A dear friend once told me I was putting him on a pedestal as if he were God. I should love myself more.

It finally registered. Sir was going to continue what he did, rob Peter to pay Paul, boast and brag and hurt his family. I fell in love with his hopes and dreams to take me to a place of paradise and reach back and pay it forward helping those less fortunate. The dream and aspiration turned into a life of trickery. Blocking out my chaotic life of abuse was what helped me survive. I needed to break away from the manipulation and dictatorship.

In order for my situation to change, I needed to change and get my power back. I made my mind up that after my youngest son graduated from high school I was going to leave. But, I needed to strengthen my mind, get closer to the Lord and interact with the outside world.

Even though he always spoke against me going to college, this was something I needed to do.

On the way home from work, I stopped at Oakland Community College and applied for a Free Application For Federal Student Aid, FAFSA, and filled out a college application. I started imagining myself in class, learning and completing an associate's degree and moving on to a university finishing up with a bachelor's degree. About a week later Sir said, "You should apply for school because the mortgage industry isn't looking like it's coming back." I was shocked! I said, "Yes, sir." I didn't tell him I already did.

I took the next step and scheduled time to take the math and English assessment needed to know what courses to register for. It was important I took my time and answered the questions correctly because the score determined what class I was placed in. I was resolute to get a four-year college education in four years, so I went full time. I didn't entertain the thought I'd been out of school for eighteen years. I didn't anticipate the struggles I would have in college.

The test anxiety I developed, I fought by asking to either take the test outside the classroom or in the resource room. I had skills already, so college wasn't to get my dream job but a nation of things. To build my self-confidence and prepare myself for my life to come; I needed to learn how to make decisions. Most importantly I wanted my children to have a better life and what better way to show them than by example.

Since, Jade was my only girl I needed to make sure I was giving her the attention she was seeking. Every night I scheduled thirty minutes with Jade. I wanted to make it quality time. We talked, read a book, or chitchatted. Thirty minutes was not enough time and it usually ran over.

I enjoyed her telling me about her day. I read a book or told her stories. We planned afterschool and summer activities. I loved going to Borden Park and sledding down the hill. Jade was a track star and I tried to race her. Not a chance for me. But in speed walking, I had her beat. She helped me plant flowers along the house. Deer would eat most of them. Bowling was fun too. But what I liked most was sitting under the large tree sprouting through the round hole cut in the center of the deck and looking at the stars.

I wanted to have a great mother-daughter relationship built on a bed of Daffodils surrounded by Amaryllis, Apple Blossoms, and Birds of Paradise.

Once a Cheater Always a Cheater

Dear Lord,

A couple years passed since the last affair I knew of, but tension was building inside me. A couple of months after my last child our intimate relations caused severe pain, tearing and bleeding, but he didn't care. We continued to have sex anyway. I didn't understand why I was in so much pain. I wondered was it the mental stress of our relationship or was it due to Sir Klyde's many affairs. I went to several doctors over the years, but no one could figure out the issue I was suffering.

When Sir constantly complimented other women and started the same behavior pattern, as before, I knew he had not gone to the pastor about his problem. But he was still acting as a pastor's armor barrier, up front taking pictures of the congregation but committing adultery and mistreating his family every chance he got.

He left his phone on the sofa next to me and when I looked through it I found a picture of a naked woman with her legs spread open and another woman standing next to his car posing. I would have seen more, but he came back into the room. He knew something was wrong; so he asked if I looked through his phone. I asked him who the women were. He denied the pictures were his. He told me his brother sent them to him and then he put a lock on his phone.

A different day but the same old stuff. It was getting old and I was on my way out when my Uncle Christopher and Aunt Ramona from Arizona came to visit, Sir spoke to them about our situation. I was shocked and impressed because he'd never spoken willingly about our problems. This was out of character so I thought he changed. Everything inside me wanted him to be different. I started to think God couldn't bless us if he kept disobeying the Word.

I felt I couldn't trust him not only because he had a sex addiction, but we were behind in all our bills including the house note. Creditors called and letters were threatening to foreclosure on our house. We were doing everything we could to save our home. We borrowed money from family, friends, employer and even a pastor. Dan Hendricks, the owner of the mortgage company Sir worked for loaned him $3,000 but Dan said I had to agree to the loan before he gave it to him.

I applied for food stamps and assistance with the utilities through the Department of Human Services. After I got home, I went upstairs to the bedroom where he sat on the bed. I sat next to him and expressed how things had not changed. I pulled out my journal and started reading how he'd treated me over the years and how things were the same. I read all the problems I had with him and the things he said he'd change. I also told him I wanted a God fearing man who didn't abuse his wife or children, but loved and cherished us the way Christ loves the church.

I told him it was unfair the way he treated the children and me. I said I needed someone who was not afraid of getting a job. The bible says if a man can't take care of his family he is worse than an infidel. I laid on the bed and turned away from him then with his foot he jammed my back and pushed me off the bed. I jumped up like a ninja, surprised and shocked. He really hadn't changed at all. The rage was still buried inside. I fought back and said, "I wish you would hit me. I'm not scared of you."

He leaped towards me knocking me to the floor twisted me in a knot and squeezed me like he was squeezing the air out of the inner tube. I refused to let this keep happening. Once he released me I ran out of the house and down to the Rochester Hills police station to file a report. I told them he was a Rochester Hills volunteer fire fighter. He kicked me off the bed, slammed me on the floor and my ankle twisted underneath me I jumped up and slapped him. The police officer said since I hit him too he was not going to file a report.

I didn't want Sir to lose his job, but I didn't want him to ever hit me again. No way was I going back. So I parked the Jeep in front of the house where three-pine trees blocked the vision of the street. I slept in the truck that night. I came into the house limping, the next morning.

He made a bath with bubbles and Epsom salt to heal my ankle. Rubbed my hair and told me he loved me. It was a little scary. He'd never made me a bath water before or given me the attention I needed. When I got out of the tub, he dried me off and me laid across the bed and massaged my back. I always asked for one back rub, but he never did it right. He'd push on my skin like I was contagious.

I was sure he was stressed over bills but being stressed should never be an excuse for abuse. I wanted a man who loved God unconditionally, prayed with his family. Led his family in a godly way. Be the head of the family and set an example on how to study and be the best child of God we could be, husband, father, son, daughter, wife, brother, sister, and friend.

I wanted a man who treated me with love and respect. Not talk to me like I was dumb or act as though I didn't know what I was talking about. When I asked a question, didn't make me feel stupid for asking. Or when I asked for the time, he'd not say look at your cell phone. If he saw me walking to the wrong car, he'd not let me continue in the wrong direction. That's mean! I wanted to have a loving caring conversation. Make decisions together and come up with solutions together.

I needed a real man who could control his flesh and take care of his family.

Our mortgage company's Saxon Mortgage payment plan was $3,500 dollars a month. But we couldn't even make a $1200 payment. He was not closing any loans, and he wouldn't get another job. Closing mortgage loan should be his hobby because it wasn't paying the bills.

I worked in the Parmount Bank mortgage department when I decided to let go of the struggle. I emailed my husband to let him know we needed to stop fighting and let the house go. Soon after, I got laid off work from the bank. The mortgage side of the bank was not doing well. I put my entire check in the bank to help save our house, but it was a losing battle.

I hadn't noticed he controlled my life down to the checking account. The sad thing was I didn't realize my debit card was missing until I saw a card with my name on it amongst his things. I was bringing home the money, but he had taken all control. Once the mortgage industry crashed I woke up and saw the light. I was stronger than I thought. I took care of my husband and three children on a thirty thousand dollar salary. What did I need a man for, I thought. Once we received a foreclosure notice I got a clearer picture how life would continue.

Every summer I planned activities for the children but this summer was different. They were getting out of school soon, and we were going to be homeless. It only took six months before our house was foreclosed. We had to move out and live hotel to hotel. We tried to get the lowest rates on Hotwire and Priceline.com.

I was hiding the fact we were homeless from my family and the church. We spent the night everywhere. I stayed at family members' home late and sometimes slept in the car in a hotel parking lot and go inside to wash up in their bathroom.

The children and I worked cutting yards for

$30 to $40 a day to have gas money and food. When I went to McDonalds, I could only buy one drink and the rest were waters. Sometimes I put a little lemonade in the cups.

I went to the food pantry at church, and one lady told me "You all are rich. You don't need anything. Stop playing." I smiled and walked out. We did need food but what was I supposed to say? We were the family who helped other families buy their first homes, refinance or to make stuff happen even moved out of the inner city into the suburbs. We'd given a car away and donated money to the church. Behind having a messed up marriage, we loved helping other people.

I wondered if were we paying the price for his infidelity. We jumped from hotel to hotel until his friend Tony, a guy Sir taught about the housing industry, let us stay in his 4200 square foot home, a five bedroom, 3 ½ baths, 2 ½ car garage. The basement was the size of the entire house. Tony only asked for us to pay the utilities.

So living rent-free, we should have been saving a lot of money. It was a nice change from sleeping in the car. This was an opportunity to build and keep our family together.

Jade's room was a suite on the other side of the home with a walk-in closet and a private bath.

The boys had their own separate rooms with a game room off the side. This was Jade's junior year in high school but the move was hard on her. Her friends were in a different school district and we still weren't communicating well.

I started having sleeping overs inviting family and children from the church. It was a great way to open up dialogue by sitting in a circle allowing the children to talk about things that bothered them. I made suggestions how to handle bullying and self-esteem.

Thanksgiving

Dear Lord,

I admit we counted on Jade a lot. She was dependable and reliable. But Thanksgiving Day she was tired of us calling on her so often. The house was full of Sir Klyde's family when he called her name and she didn't come. He searched the house and found her hiding under the bed. He picked her up, threw her body against the wall breaking the drywall. Then dragged her to a second story window and threaten to throw her out; all because she did not come when he called for her.

Everybody watched what happened, but nobody said anything. Needless to say, this Thanksgiving dinner ended abruptly. Maybe they thought they were saying something by leaving. It was a statement, maybe. I stood by helpless. I guess they did too.

He'd gotten more public with his displays of anger, allowing his entire family to witness his outage. There was always an excuse to justify his behavior. I didn't understand how some people thought putting their hands on their children was a way of controlling them and keeping them in their place.

I wasn't physically abused as much anymore, but my Jade was. I had to save my family. Sir Klyde's sister Lily consoled her by singing a song to help her get through the pain and embarrassment. I went to her and asked why was she hiding. Definitely not the right thing to say after you were beaten up. I didn't know the right words because she was getting the abuse I used to get. I told her I was sorry, prayed for her and told her God would take care of her.

Like always I never witnessed the attacks first hand. Sir told me his interpretation of what happened. I didn't believe him because I knew it didn't take much to set him off. I had an uncomfortable feeling like a gag in my mouth because I was not protecting her. I needed to do something, but I felt I had to keep getting stronger first.

Sir Klyde's family distanced themselves from him, but he continued as though nothing happened. We stayed out of his way to avoid conformation. I was setting a bad example for her and the boys allowing this abuse to go on.

I was teaching her to accept abuse or be an abuser.

After the Thanksgiving incident, Jade was angry and confused. She asked how could her dad put his hands on her like that, she was his only daughter. Her dad's side of the family tried to get her to leave with them but of course he said, NO!

Everyone was confused because she never screamed but in my mind it would have only made matters worse, especially since he threatened to throw her out the second floor window. The thing that hurt her most was the next day after church. Sir Klyde's little sister, Jade and I were at my mother's house. Sitting at the table, we were talking about the night before when I asked why was she in his way. The thing is, I didn't remember saying those words to her. I hurt her more than when her dad beat her up. She thought I would understand how she felt since the domestic violence started with me.

Jade didn't talk much about the night. She wanted to forget. But after she read the first draft of this book she shared some of her pain. I would not have known how she felt about that night if I hadn't written this story. I was hurt and in pain by what Jade felt during the Thanksgiving incident.

I was in such a fog and in a battered woman syndrome that I really missed the effects the abuse had on me. I'd become a silencer, a woman in denial. I was so oblivious to the side effect of what abuse had on children.

I'm so sorry I didn't realize how I had destroyed our mother daughter relationship. I tried to figure it out, the answer was right in front of me.

.

"Turn Wounds into Wisdom."

Oprah Winfrey

Chapter 10
NO MORE EXCUSES

Dear Lord,

I was blessed to meet a lady who was a counselor helped children in high school take basic college courses during the summer of their eleventh grade year. Jade took the same basic English and math assessment test I did when I applied for college. Jade was accepted and the counselor guided my daughter to select the courses needed to prepare her for college.

One of the courses was a college art class. I was still taking college courses and needed a humanity class. I was able to take a course with her, thus completing my associate's degree in liberal arts. I couldn't remember the last time we had that much fun together. We started a t-shirt design business and rented a booth at a church convention at COBO Hall. I felt empowered and we were a team.

Her desire and inspiration to create art was beautiful. Her passion was divine. I watched the posture of her hand as she stroked her pencil against her pad, mentally absorbing the model before transposing it in onto her pad. She wanted to catch not just every detail but the very essence of her subject... And I loved it.

During that year, we received a note on the door, a foreclosure notice. The owner of the home stopped making the mortgage payments, which I was unaware of. Homeless again! Same old thing just a different day. Hotel hopping and not knowing where we were going to sleep was getting tiresome. When my patience wore thin, a job opening at IEE Automotive USA, an engineering company became available. I was hired by IEE as a Test Subject there.

The engineers suggested I apply for the student-engineering position. I was not even in school for engineering, but for business. I had no experience in engineering. However, I applied for the job immediately. On a Friday, the interviewer told me the student position paid $10.00 an hour. She asked me what I thought and I told her I was thinking $15.00. She shook my hand and told me she would get back to me. Before the end of the day, she called and said, "The offer was accepted. How soon can you start?"

The following Monday I started working at IEE as a part time quality control intern but worked full time. On the home front, we were having a hard time finding an apartment without a co-signer. So getting hired was perfect timing. Sir Klyde's old co-worker was moving to Hawaii. The mortgage business was still not great but better. He was asking $1700 a month for a three-bedroom condo. I knew we couldn't afford it, but I was tired of being on the streets. The first couple of months I worked full time making my monthly checks equal $1700 a month.

But after a few months, my hours were cut back to part time. I couldn't afford to pay the rent in full anymore. We were four months behind and have to move out or find a way to pay this man his money.

We were close to the move out date and school was almost out for the summer. I prayed Sir would find another place to live before the time came.

I started planning ahead, getting rid of almost everything even our Christmas tree. I made several trips to the local Salvation Army. I saw no need to procrastinate and prolong the inevitable.

I went to work every day and left Sir at home. He worked out of the condo but never closed loans. When we first moved, he cleaned the house and had dinner waiting. I loved it. I brought the money home and he took care of the house. I complimented him often. I wasn't sure if the compliments or the fact he wasn't making any money made him stop.

I asked him why he stopped cooking, but he never could give me a good answer. Because "I'm working" was not good enough. If I'd known he wasn't going to be able to contribute and we would be homeless. I wouldn't have bought a Honda Accord for $14,000 with a $328 monthly payment. I would have settled for the Honda Civic at $5,000. I was glad I didn't get the $18,000 Altima, even though I liked it more.

However, here we were again in search of somewhere to live. He was stressed but if he got a real job, he'd feel better.

While I stood folding clothes on my bed, Sir came in and started hassling me. As he continued to talk, he got louder and louder. He always came home and found fault in something, anything, didn't matter what.

Jade came downstairs from her bedroom and

closed the door while he was yelling at me. After he finished with me, he went into Jade's room and told her don't ever touch his door.

I yelled out, "What do you mean? That was the right thing to do. She should have closed the door. We should have closed the door. Leave her alone." The children didn't need to hear us arguing. Children should never be involved in adult problems. I went into her room and apologized to her and told her it was going to be okay.

After the incident with Jade, he was at it again. I couldn't pretend everything was okay anymore, I couldn't. I knew it was a lot of stress due to a lack of money and being homeless, but it was no excuse for his behavior.

It took two weeks to build up enough courage to talk to him. I went into the family room where the children were watching television. I said, "I'm going to talk to Daddy about abusing you all." I promised he was not going to touch them, not to be scared. And he would not hurt them. They said, "No, Mom. He's only going deny it." I said it's okay. "I'm fed up. We can't keep living in fear."

I went into our bedroom with a stern and serious tone. I let Sir know we're going to have a conversation about abusing our children.

We needed to talk about what happened with the children a couple of weeks ago. I wanted to hear what he had to say. Sir told me they tried to step up on him and disrespect him. He picked up Ja'vian only once and threw him down. And pushed Ja'von in the chest and he dramatized it and fell into the wall. "See you weren't there to see it. You are taking their side," he said.

I didn't believe him. He picked up Ja'vian several times and slammed him on the ground for not picking up a piece of Nerds candy. Because I was in the next room when he socked Ja'von in his chest many times, I heard doom, doom, doom, doom, like the ceiling was caving in. When I ran into the kitchen Ja'von was lodged partly inside the drywall. Sir said, "It's not what you think. He tripped and fell."

I didn't believe anything he told me anymore. I called the children into the bedroom. I told Sir they are going to talk freely and he was not going to yell or hit them. I called the boys in the room, as they stood at the bedroom entryway emotionless like stones. I told them to nod their heads if they'd agreed with what I was saying. They glanced at me as to say 'no, Mom I can't do this.' I was determined to stop the abuse. But Sir told me I didn't know what I was talking about. As he stood, I saw the anger all over him. His lips pulled together tight, nose flared and fist balled. "I will do whatever I want to them and you can't stop me," he said.

This stance was all too familiar, like a bull ready to attack. It was most scary when it was a sneak attack and he caught you off guard. I stood disguising my fear, told the children to leave the room. We continued to talk about our relationship as a whole I told him he was rude and disrespectful to the children and me.

He expressed anger and didn't know how to respond to my boldness so he attacked me by saying I'm worthless and good for nothing and I couldn't satisfy him sexually. He went hard by stating if I had health insurance my panani wouldn't be broke, except he used a more graphic word. I told him he was selfish and if he loved me, he wouldn't force himself on me.

How could a husband say such hurtful words to his wife. Someone he should love unconditionally. Instead, he tore me down and ripped me apart. He as the man, the head of this household, was supposed to take care of his family, not the other way around. I told him once before if he wanted to stay at home and take care of the house and children that's fine. I would be the breadwinner. No pressure. I couldn't be both. Not if I had a man, a husband. He wanted everyone to believe he was the best husband and father but look how he treated us.

It was clear he only cared about yourself. I couldn't do this anymore. "I want a divorce!" Sir shocked me when he said, "Oh yeah, I would have gotten one a long time ago but I couldn't afford it and it's cheaper to keep you."

Wow, that was how he really felt. I realized worrying about how Sir felt about me and the way I allowed him to treat me did not take away tomorrow's troubles, but did take away today's peace.

I started researching storage units and living arrangements. I had to stop accepting anything and start living the way God intended. I was going to file Chapter 7 on my life. Completely purge and start over.

Since he saw how serious I was, he decided counseling was the answer. I did not want counseling. After a couple months, it was time to take it to the next level and get intimate. Hold up wait a minute. Stop the record sort of speak. "No, it's too soon. I'm not ready," I said. Nothing has changed. I couldn't get passed him saying my panani was broke and I needed to fix it. Things were not better. Sex was not an option. The marriage counselors said okay. Gave us tapes to listen to and a homework assignment. Practice communication, compliment each other and start physical contact, hug and hold hands.

The next week we sat in their living room, two chairs facing north and two chairs facing south. As we faced the marriage counselors they prayed and the wife said, "We have a few scriptures I want us to read." She started reading from the bible and suddenly I felt an overwhelming emotional ache in my chest. I didn't know why was I being affected. We were here to help Sir not me. Tears rolled down my face like a waterfall. I couldn't stop crying. They kept reading.

I felt a release from heavy pressure weighing down on me. I didn't know. I didn't realize I needed help too. I looked at Sir, hugged him and told him, "I forgive you." But as I cried I heard a voice *you are released you are free, you know what you have to do now.* NO more excuses. I walked out of the session free of the years of heartache and pain. God allowed me to see what I needed to see.

I wanted my marriage to work so badly I accepted anything, almost anything he dished out. He talked a good game and I fell for the Okie Dokie. I took responsibility for my decisions. I accepted the fits of rage, the outburst of anger, the emotional and physical abuse. It was something I couldn't overcome on my own.

I didn't know fully why my family members were divorced, but I knew I needed to break the abusive cycle I allowed for so many years.

I realized I had settled for less. A real man doesn't abuse his family. My daddy taught me no man should ask a woman for money. My daddy said, "You can do bad by yourself. But usually you do better because you can have money in your pocket and a peace of mind. Don't worry about the dumb stuff." In order to live I had to forgive.

My mom said I could stay with her, but it was too far from my job. My aunt and uncle owned a woman's shelter and my children and I moved into New Bethel Women's Shelter. I went to work every day as though nothing was going on and I went to church on Sundays and Tuesdays.

Jade graduated from Troy High and was accepted in Ferris State University. I'd figure out everything later. Jade had a heart of gold. She had a passion for helping those in need. She would give the clothes off her back.

I paid more attention to her now. My sister told me she needed me and always had. It was my love she was seeking. I couldn't see it. But now I do. I love my daughter and I wanted her to grow up happy. A happy child grows up to be a happy adult.

We started communicating better and experienced new things together. I loved how our new relationship was developing.

Sir picked up a U-Haul to load the condo and move our things to the storage unit off Dequindre and Avon in Rochester Hills. While Jade and I packed the U-Haul, he stood around and talked on the phone. He let two 110 lb. women pick up full and queen size beds, dressers and a 5-drawer vertical file cabinet.

The Night of July 4th

Dear Lord,

I was mentally gone and physically weak. I couldn't continue to ignore or refuse to deal with this lifestyle. Klyde knew I was moving to the shelter with the children, but I had the sense to not let Klyde know I was planning to leave for good. Staying in the shelter prepared me for what life would be without violence. In the early morning I left the shelter, drove around Rochester looking for homes for rent. I found one I liked, but was led not to say anything, I remember like it was yesterday-- celebrating Independence Day in Bellville at Sir Klyde's parents' house.

Everything was going well. The food was good and family fellowship was great. It was close to 10:00 p.m. Sir and I were leaning against his car talking. He said, "I'm tired of the way Jade treats Ja'von. I'm going inside and tell her Ja'von has to go with her to the movies or she can't go." I agreed. I waited outside thinking it would only take a second.

About six minutes later I had a horrifying

flashback. My daughter Jade and her boyfriend Remmi ran out of her grandparents' house screaming and crying for dear life. I felt her pain. "I yelled what happened? Tell me what happened!" As she approached me screaming I saw her dad burst through the front door of the house. All I could say was "GO! GO! GO!"   Lock the doors I knew that look, the evil streaming from his eyes. They jumped in her boyfriend car and backed into my green Honda Accord. I yelled "Roll the windows up lock the doors, I don't care about the car, just GO! GO! GO!" Sir ran up to the door grabbed the handle and banged on the window.

He ran up to me huffing and puffing. "Why did you let her go? She hit me. She hit *me*." I looked at him in disbelief and said, "No, she didn't." I didn't want to hear it. I looked away from him and said, "Who else was there, who can tell me what happened?" Sir Klyde's sister came outside. "You witness this?" I asked.

Lily said, "I did."

I said, "Okay, tell me what happened."

It was as I thought. He lost control, grabbed her throat, picked her up off her feet and threw her against the wall and started choking her. The initial reaction was slow to rescue her. It was a shock to everyone in the room. She was helpless. It took five adults to pry his hands from her throat.

I couldn't imagine a father harming his daughter. When he told me it was self-defense I looked at him, cocked my head and said, "Really?" That was the best he could come up with. Pleading temporary insanity would have been more believable. I knew something was wrong with him. On a good day, he could make me feel like he's my best friend and the world was peachy cream and everything was going to be all right. But at the drop of a dime he could be my worst nightmare. He showed people what he wanted them to see. It was crazy, but his closest friends didn't know what he was capable of. Chocking Jade confirmed I made the right decision. My daughter went to the police station, and reluctantly pressed charges.

The next day I called the landlord, told him I wanted to move in right away. I picked up the keys and moved into a new two-bedroom town home in downtown Rochester. Jade made a police report and the state handled the case. Jade didn't want her dad to get in trouble; she wanted him to get help. He was sentenced probation and anger management.

The Day Our Adventure Started

August 28, 2008

Jade and I went on a road trip to Northern Michigan University. It was precious. We drove from Rochester Hills, through Flint, and Grand Blanc. Eventually, we came to the Mackinac Island Bridge and it was terrifying.

I pulled over at the entrance of the bridge. The bridge looked to me like a giant scary dragon. It was intimidating and unforgiving. It wasn't because of the water beneath the bridge. It was that dragon breathing cold and wet fire.

I looked to Jade and she looked at me like I knew better than to even ask. A patrolman sat in a car alongside the bridge. I looked at the bridge not knowing what we were going to do when I noticed people were walking to the patrolman. They were asking him to drive over that dragon because they must know a fire-breathing dragon when they see one too.

I asked him if he could help us. I never heard of such a thing but from the line of cars waiting for the bridge patrolman, he was asked a lot.

The countryside was beautiful. We pulled over and took pictures. We passed an area that looked like a movie set from the Wild Wild West. We arrived eight hours later. Our GPS took us right to the vicinity of the school but not to the exact location. Marquette was a small, quaint town with beautiful old buildings.

As we stood in the elevator of Northern University's school administration building, Jade said: "Mom we look like sisters so don't tell anyone you're my mother because they gonna think you had me when you were two."

We headed to student housing. Jade was the first to arrive in her dorm room. She was able to choose which side she wanted. She was really happy about that.

After getting settled into her new space, we went on a shopping extravaganza for everything she needed. We bought a lot of winter stuff, scarves, gloves and dri-fit socks so she'd be prepared for what we both knew would be a harsh northern Michigan winter.

We walked the campus so Jade could get acclimated to her new surroundings. The art building was absolutely amazing. The structure of the building itself was made of glass and they had a classroom for every subject: ceramics, animation, and graphic design – each room catered in design to its subject. It felt like a museum.

Some dorm rooms were new. Hers wasn't. Some hallways were gothically dark while others were fluorescently bright. We finished settling for the night and I picked up my diary and started to write. I noticed Jade watching me with tears in her eyes and began to weep. I said, "Jade, what's wrong? We've had such a beautiful day!"

She told me through tears, "Mom – I wouldn't be going to college if it weren't for you." And I started crying, too.

Upper Michigan had a lot of areas to bike and hike. We went to Sugar Loaf – a public park. They had a lot of trails and overhanging rock on a boulder-strewn hillside. Jade and I walked a path with mountains on both sides. We climbed the steep side to feed our hunger to explore. Some checkpoints were difficult to climb.

We stumbled, tripped and posed all along the uphill journey. The texture of the mountain was moist, colorful and amazing. We made it to the top of the big overhang on the lake. We posed for pictures. The view was absolutely amazing. Climbing the mountain together – that was worth the trip.

Jade told me of a restaurant that turned into a

club at night. Before 11:00 p.m., they allowed in students eighteen years old. After 11:00, it was twenty-one and older. It was the only place Marquette had for people to unwind. I was skeptical about going at first because I had not been in a club since 1991 and the thought of me in a club with my daughter seemed strange and unsettling.

Jade wouldn't let the club idea go; she wanted me to be happy and have some fun with her. I finally agreed. She introduced me to her roommate and some other students in the dorm. One of her friends was in cosmetology school. Jade had her do my hair and another girl did my makeup while she picked out the clothes I was to wear. I felt like a beauty queen being pampered and groomed.

I met some of her male friends who were football players and boxers. They seemed very nice and polite - the way they pleasantly smiled and shook my hand as they greeted me.

We all went to the afterhours club. We danced and danced. Jade moved her hips up and down and dropped them. The dance was called hip roll. All I could do was the Stanky Leg dance by GS Boyz. I got such a crowd around me I didn't know how to act. This was my first time dancing since I was eighteen years old and I was sharing the experience with a young lady that used to be my baby.

I will admit my rhythm was a little off. Jade was laughing at me. However, all the Caucasian people appeared to like it. They asked me if I could teach them to move like me. Jade couldn't believe it. They made a "stanky leg" circle around me. Jade, all the while, was cracking up. I had so much fun.

Discovering Me

Dear Lord,

What began as an innocent relationship spiraled into an abusive roller coaster. I only wanted to be loved. I cut out the outside world, and lost my identity and sense of purpose. I had to save my children and worry about me later. I valued my children's lives over my own.

I'd always heard that children were better off in a two-parent household. Children are better with a father that's not the best, rather than having no father at all. I came to realize that is not true.

Staying in an abusive relationship was unhealthy; in fact it did much more harm than good in my situation.

The question many have asked me, is why did I stay so long. The reason I endured the pain is not a simple answer. There are many facets to my answer, one being marriage, and they were sacred to me. I wanted desperately for my children to be raised in a two-parent household. I didn't want to let the church down. People looked up to us. I wanted to break the generation curse of divorces in my family. The quest to prove my family wrong consumed me. I'd invested so many years, I didn't want to throw them away. Also, I didn't know if he'd try to hurt me if I left and I was afraid of the unknown.

I hit rock bottom when I felt I couldn't protect my family and I had lost the battle. I watched movies on abuse and finally got to the point where I decided I was not going to be a statistic, end in up dead, or in jail. I needed to come up with an exit plan, a plan of escape even if this was not what I wanted. I needed to be prepared. "Live for the moment but plan for the future."

I had to be careful and calculate every move. Abusers are unpredictable so standing up to him could be dangerous. Leaving may not be the best option.

I needed to rebuild my self-confidence and self-worth with as little friction as possible in order to have the courage to leave. I was isolated and needed to get involved with the outside world. Church and school events became my social outlet. I was shot down for investing so much time in church, but I knew I had to stand on solid ground.

Abuse was killing me slowly. A month before the

July 4th incident I spoke to my aunt about getting out of my situation. She told me about a women's shelter she and my uncle owned. She informed me I had options and didn't need to stay in a dangerous place. New Bethel Women's shelter had two beds available for my children and me,

The shelter for battered and abused woman and children was the best option for me. I stayed four weeks and overcame my dependency, the strong hold Sir had over me.

There are agencies around the country, in every city, that provide food and shelter for woman and children. While, in the shelter, I qualified for food assistance, which allowed me to help some of the other woman and children with items the shelter didn't provide. With the agency's help, I was able to pay first month's rent and security deposit on a townhome where I began my new, independent life.

I was fortunate to have a job. Being financially independent was one of the most powerful things I had. I opened a separate bank account and hid the documents.

It's my suggestion even if you decide not to leave, build your confidence, prepare to be financially stable and self-sufficient. These are power tools no one can take from you. If not a job, go to school and learn a trade.

It was a long process, building and uplifting myself. Coming out of an elusive dream state, I was wakened. Change was constant. Change came in slow motion. I didn't realize the change happened until it was over.

I challenged what I feared--being alone, unmarried, a single woman raising children by myself and in fear of being a statistic. Knowing this was not the life God intended for me. Realizing there was a bigger picture, bigger than Sir, bigger than me. I chose to live at the highest vibration; my commitment to purpose and self-respect for my children, others, and myself deepened my soul. Letting go of bondage released me to mend, heal, and conquer...!

I had to change in order for my situation to change and move forward. I took off my mask and showed myself to the world. Most importantly, I had to be restored on the inside to be transformed on the outside. To help motivate me, I had to change my mindset. Words have power to build and destroy. I chose to build. Focus on now and move forward, let the past be the past

I forgave myself; abandoned the spirit of denial and released a defensive mindset, allowing me to accentuate the positive. I set a new standard. I strengthened my mind, body, and soul through prayer, mediation yoga, student counseling, and exercise.

I learned love was not abuse. I didn't deserve to be abused; I deserved better. Since Jade and I had such an explosive relationship, we needed help. I embraced her with love and we both sought counseling to build ourselves.

Once we broke through the storm, I discovered me. I opened my eyes, looked in the mirror and said, "Hello there!" During my marriage, I thought it selfish to cater to my needs. I was a caregiver by nature. I loved it. I desired to help those in need. What I found was I was in need also. I started loving myself, which in turn helped me love my children better.

I started getting my hair done on a weekly basis. It was not only therapeutic but also away to boost my self-esteem. I appreciate Tracie Hair Salon for being a faith based hair ministry with affordable prices. She is a true servant of God.

I am no longer blinded by the fictitious notion of a family curse. I'm released from caring about statistic and having a baby's daddy. I honor and respect myself. I know my worth. I don't live to please a man. I love myself. I understand my strength. I will not rush into a relationship again but take my time and wait on God.

Having a clear mind allowed me to make better decisions. I now choose wisely who I allow into my life. Most importantly I learned how to lean and depend on the word of God.

My mother always told me, "Don't take life for granted! Tomorrow is not promised to you. Take the reins and don't give anyone else power over you. If a guy hits you once, get out, He will do it again. You are not a doormat. You are queen in Christ Jesus." My mother was right!

The healing process after I left wasn't what I anticipated. I thought it would be an easy transition. During the honeymoon separation and preparation period of the divorce was a sense of enlightenment. I felt elated and on a cloud of its own in a blissful state of being. I deserved a life where I could be happy, not live in fear. But once the deal was sealed and the divorce was final I went through a bout of depression.

I couldn't imagine what was to come. The rumors ran rampant in the church. I was accused of spreading lies about my in-laws and sharing our family business with the world when in fact I was quiet and didn't want anyone to know, especially the church.

The ones dearest to me, my sisters-in-law turned

their backs on me. My mother-in-law shunned me. I received a cold shoulder by a minister at church who was best friends with my mother-in-law. I never looked at them as an outsider but as part of my family. I was isolated in my world but free from eminent danger. I didn't want to sugarcoat anything but to be honest in sharing my story.

I was the queen of disguise, so I thought. My actions said otherwise. Family noticed me losing control of my children and I was making careless mistakes at work. I thought I was handling things well but I was clearly not.

I prayed for God's help. My family, aunts, uncles and cousins were emotionally supportive. My mother and my sister Soni allowed me to store our personal items in their homes, and made sure we were a part of family outings. They encouraged me by way of scripture and with their love and support.

Much love and support came through my co-workers, Oakland University and the Oakland Community College. Polly a coworker and I would workout together. Physical exercise was great for the brain. Yoga class taught me the techniques of breathing and how to clear my mind of clutter.

Dale, a coworker, took me out and showed me how a lady should be treated. My co-workers took care of my car, changed my oil and replaced my old set of tires for a brand new set of tires. I felt loved and protect by my coworkers at IEE automotive.

I reached out for student counseling at Oakland University and took classes on self-esteem and personal assertiveness at Oakland Community College. I practiced what I learned in everyday life. While in counsel, scriptures was my aid in the time of need. I searched the bible for keywords and used them to uplift me.

Part of my healing became "all about me." I had to love myself before anyone else could. The mirror was taboo for me I never looked in it. I thought it was vain and took too much of my time.

I looked at myself in the mirror then told myself I like myself until it flowed with no problem into I love myself. I like my hair to I love my hair. Being able to get my hair done often was key to how I saw myself. It made me feel good.

I released the fear. Abuser: he was less than a man to have placed his hands on children and me. He couldn't get in right in twenty years what makes me think he could ever do it. I told him he has low self-esteem and in order to build himself up he torn me down, in private not in public. He destroyed the relationship but I allowed it to go on. I had the control of what I allowed in my bubble and I chose me.

As I felt better about myself and learned my self-worth I got stronger, I started to let my light shine and let God use me.

A job opportunity came about at Duke University Medical Center as a General Manager in Durham, North Carolina. My family was in full support and they let me know it would be okay to come back if I needed to. I know I should not feel alienated, that they love me and would support me either way.

I moved to North Carolina meeting Word Empowerment first lady Lady Suzette who took me under her wing. Pastor Apostle Spence at WE church spoke to my soul. "Mom, it's like he's talking directly to you," my son said. They became my spiritual guidance once I left Michigan. My pastor back home also showed genuine concern and prayed for my soul.

By the way, my suggestion to anyone being abused, call the police anytime he or she hits you! If no one knows your being abused no one can help you.

I was glad I leaned and depended on the Lord myself, not allowing outsiders to influence my decision to leave Sir. The Lord was my sole provider, my comforter in a time of need. When I was lonely, he held me tight. In my darkest hour, I called on the name of Jesus. His word sustained me.

Drinking to an intoxicated state led to bad decisions, getting me into a situations I should not have been in. But thank you, Lord, for seeing me through and living to tell my story.

I truly see; my eyes are opened wide, the blindfold lifted. I owe it to the faithfulness of God's word.

Writing Daffodil has been therapeutic for us. We've discussed things from the past that were taboo. We opened up and shared our most intimate thoughts that brought us closer. Every day we'd end up talking about our relationship as mother and daughter. After the first draft, I decided we needed a Pamper Me day.

"You can step up, speak up, and break away from violence. There is grace under fire, God is in control."

House Rules

Once I snapped out of depression I became consistent in the way I handled things and placed a note on the front door stating,

1. This is a smoke & alcohol free home.
2. If I smell a hint of smoke- You're not coming in.
3. If I (Ms. Strong) don't know you, don't come in.
4. If you are a female and Ms. Strong is not here, do not enter under any circumstances.
5. If you don't take your shoes off, *don't* come in.
6. If any part of this house in or out is not clean there will be consequences.
7. If you eat here, clean/wash your own dish.
8. Don't leave any mess for someone else to clean- Do it yourself.
9. There will be no more in-house wrestling.
10. If another thing of mine gets broken whomever is here will be responsible to pay/replace it.
11. NO one is allowed to spend the night without prior approval.

12. For those who reside here (siblings) at 310 N. Alice Ave. who can't get along will be forced to move out.

13. I will no longer tolerate the mistreatment of anyone.

14. No foul language of any sort- especially the N word.

15. Homework will be done everyday.

16. Cell phones will be shut off at 11pm.

17. Get to school and every class on time.

18. Dinner is at 9pm or otherwise stated.

19. Everyone who sleeps and use this address will be responsible for chores.

20. Prepare for school each night.

21. Everyone sixteen years and older are required to contribute to the household.

22. If you are over eighteen years old your curfew is midnight unless prior arrangements are made with the leaseholder (me).

Mirror Mirror"

Dear Lord,

Now that I snapped out of the fog I know my daughter needs me. I didn't think I mattered as much because I was always there. But with your help, Lord, Jade listens to me. It didn't happen over night. We both wanted a better relationship and now we communicate without arguing.

Jade loves helping me pick outfits and she says to an old lady "Mom, that's not right. Here try this." Or "Can I do your hair?" She wants her mom to look her best.

As she grows and learns herself, she treats herself better and her brothers. We go out on outings together and fix meals together. I am so proud of her upward journey. I see amazing things happening. I taught my daughter to look in the mirror and say I love myself, over and over and say I love my hair. Whatever makes you feel uncomfortable about yourself, face it and change it.

I did not look at myself in the mirror. I thought putting on makeup as carnalness and a waste of time. Years went by without looking in the mirror.

Jade and I go out now. We love being around each other. Once a month is "Jade Day" where we take a day to pamper ourselves, watch a movie or go on a day trip.

I am glad I wasn't too old to learn how important it was to uproot a negative seed, and a positive seed needs watering. In addition, I learned a healthy environment must include people who will support, encourage, challenge and stimulate my mind. I started building a support system based on where I intended to go.

"You can't forgive without loving. And I don't mean sentimentality. I don't mean mush. I mean having enough courage to stand up and say, 'I forgive. I'm finished with it." Maya Angelou

Chapter 11
DAFFODIL

Jade my precious daughter,

I love you with all my heart. I thought our relationship was getting better. I listened, prayed and studied the word of God seeking guidance. But I still couldn't hear what I needed to hear.

Please forgive me for not being there when you needed me the most. The hurt and pain you experienced by the boogeyman was unthinkable and heartbreaking. I never wanted you to experience the pain that I did. I was supposed to be there to protect you. You should never be denied. I understand now why you hurt so badly, the pain, the fear, and the outcry. It was a mother's love that was supposed to protect you from the boogeyman. Nothing is worse than being betrayed by someone you love so dearly. Remember, right now, today and tomorrow the blood of Jesus protects you. We will work together for total deliverance from our past hurts.

I see serious side effects from staying in an abusive relationship. Unfortunately, some of which you've already experienced. Our mother daughter relationship has ended with lasting cramps and muscle spasms; like a migraine that won't go away.

All along you've been seeking my attention but I've been blinded by my own chaotic life almost numb to life itself-- living in an imaginary world fooling myself everything is okay, trying to make sense of my existence. I wanted to believe everything was going to be all right.

I finally heard what you were trying to tell me all along. I deserve better, I didn't have to settle, you felt my pain and wanted it to stop. I see you suffered more than I imagined. Looking back over the years, I see how my suffering affected you. Jade, I apologize for not protecting you. With all my might, I tried to stop the generational curse I felt ran through my family.

I thought I could change dad or at least change the situation. I thought staying in this dysfunctional relationship wasn't bad because you had both parents living together. But you have been abused and mistreated not only by dad but me too and there's no excuse for that. I overlooked your cries, your acts of mischievousness.

I promise you I'll overlook no more. I can tell you a thousand times how much I love you, but actions speak louder than idle words. I'm determined to stop, stand, and listen for instruction from God and express my love through a loud roar of affection. I will be a better mother. I will fight for you, for us, to have a mother daughter relationship we are destined to have.

Dear Lord,

How can we create a daffodil moment of peace, forgiveness and a new beginning? What can we do to build and repair our broken hearts and build our relationship?

I had to counteract the side effects by forgiving. Let's call it "**Daffodil**" A mother daughter journey care plan.

During my journey of heartbreak, mental and physical pain I learned to forgive.

Being motivated to change, the willingness to forgive and being able to reposition myself are critical factors in Daffodil.

Being in an abusive relationship was like a drug addiction. You think you can handle it, but you can't. I needed a twelve-step treatment plan to get out of a vital relationship and heal. The most important thing in my life beside the LORD was having peace of mind and making sure I repaired my relationship with my daughter.

Daffodil Care Plan: Creating a healthy environment to forgive, heal and start a new beginning. Jade and I cut words and pictures that represented our past, present and future. Searching through magazines, and newspapers and posting them on our walls has been therapeutic.

> "It's not an easy journey, to get to a place where you forgive people. But it is such a powerful place, because it frees you." Tyler Perry

This is only the beginning of our journey. More is yet to come. Thank You Lord in advance for your healing power!

TO MY JADE

This letter has taken an extraordinary journey finding the approximate words to demonstrate my love. I have all along known one day I would share my story with you and under what conditions I went through. Also, I wanted to penetrate your thoughts so you know how much I love you.

I believe the Lord will fight all our battles. And not put anything on us we cannot bare:

You saw the blunt of the abuse and received it yourself. I found myself empty floating in a space of existence ... so were you.

You were released to be free, to have peace of mind, and to start healing. I (we) survived!

I have made many mistakes in the past. I'll be surprised if I don't make a few more before I perish. I have learned to accept responsibly for the role I played in my life. To forgive myself first then apologize for any hurt or pain I may have caused you. You may not be able to control all life events that affect you, but you can control your point of view.

Keep this in mind as you take your extraordinary journey--the true battle is self-validation and internal congruence. Winning over your own heart and mind is what makes the difference between an unfulfilled or purposeful life. Stay steadfast and unmovable. No need to worry, I will protect you with tender love and care, forever.

Always remember your nurturing, delightful, and charming spirit will build and uplift others. God is the universe who brings it all together.

Have a positive outlook towards yourself, brothers, family, and life. For your mother knows you are designed in the image of him.

I love you with all my heart. I hope this letter of love and affection expresses my eternal love for you.

IT'S YOUR JOURNEY NOW!

My beloved

Jade: beware of those who come in a disguise as a friend who will cloud your judgment and bring confusion into your world, preventing you from reaching your full potential. You will be at a standstill. Break loose and release the shackles. Slowly open your blinded eyes and let the sunlight shine through.

Your achievements will be beyond measure. Capture and retain the essence of intelligence. Release the rough protective outer shell. Let go of the defensive demeanor that comes across abrasive at times. You are a princess preparing to be a queen. Every step is in a divine order critiqued for greatness.

Prayer to my Heavenly Father

Dear Lord, I pray you give my daughter the strength she needs to overcome her past. Implant positive thoughts in her mind. She is beautiful. Not only does she possess outer beauty but inner beauty, as well. You have designed her in the image of a beautiful flower with a ray of sunshine glowing all around her. Her understanding of why people gravitate towards her beauty is uncertain. But, you are the guide and light for her and others.

Show her destiny, Lord. Her kind hearted, sweet, impressionable and sincere personality manifest divine light and bathe all who interact with her. Build confidence in him.

An Abundance of Love

Thank you, Lord, you answered my prayers. I didn't know when it happened, but you did. I hold my daughter in my arms. I tell her I love her. Now, our channel of communication has been restored. I am free. My mind is clear. I'm getting stronger and healthier. Everything about me is getter better. My natural strength is restored and made whole.

The Illusive dream has past me by. It feels as though the negative cloud is now a lifetime away from me. You delivered me. I always wanted a life where Jade could talk openly and freely as mother and daughter should.

I look at her and feel an abundance of love radiating between us. I appreciate her, as I never have. I have had a life shift. Our relationship is blossoming to an unbreakable bond.

I know now I have a healthy environment with people who support, encourage, challenge and stimulate my mind.

I've learned to translate the negative energy from my relationship with Sir into a spiritual journey. I am now coming to realize prayer, fasting, faith and the pursuit to know you more as God is all

I needed. It outweighs the negative burdens of the world. I am still learning how to be the mother I need to be. I know I have only scratched the surface of what is to come. My daughter means the world to me. She's my best friend.

My prayer at night: thank you, Lord, for waking me this morning, for guiding and protecting me each and every day. You are Alpha and the Omega, the King of Peace. The head of my life today, tomorrow, and forevermore, you are my everything! Lead me; guide me in the direction you want me to go. Protect me from the seen and unseen that may occur. Please continue to give me strength, wisdom, and discernment in my mind, body, and soul.

Please, help me show Jade no matter what my struggles are in life, I deeply love her unconditionally.

Thank you for showing me what it means to self-love. Not to depend on anyone else to bring me joy. Joy comes from within. I've learned destruction is everywhere. Many times the person closest to you is the one who hurts you the most.

Drama and confusion consumed my life. I knew there was a higher purpose for my life.

Lord, you have always been a light in my life, my counselor, and my shoulder to cry on in the time of need. I refuse to get dragged back into confusion.

My daddy use to always say, "Don't worry about the dumb stuff, have peace of mind."

Sir Klyde's fits of rage and low self-esteem were unchangeable. I couldn't continue or ignore the issues or refuse to deal with them. I can only change myself and I chose life.

I will set a new standard for myself. I recognized my mindset needed to change and stop letting drama and negativity occupy my space.

I've shaken off the negativity, the shame and hurt. My love releases pain and suffering and brings love, joy, and peace of mind my father always spoke about.

My daughter is sweet natured, an incredible kindness and adorable sense of humor that could melt an iceberg. She's smart; gorgeous; lovable; intelligent and a beautiful person. And best of all; She is the perfect blend of wonder, warmth, joy and love. I'm proud to say she's my daughter!

THE *DAFFODIL* EXIT STRATEGY

I don't know what my future holds, but I have learned from the past and will not suffer as we did. I have a plan of action to get away from an abusive situation. I pray that my life will never come to this, but I'm prepared.

1. Develop an exit strategy on how to escape; inform a trusted friend, neighbor, family member, and coworker in advance. Send a text with a code word if in trouble.
2. Keep the phone number to your local battered women's shelter on hand.
3. Go to a doctor or emergency room if injured, report what happened to you. Tell the truth and make sure the visit is documented and take pictures of physical abuse.
4. I kept a journal noting dates, events, and threats made.
5. Identify a place to be safe and feel protected.
6. Keep car keys close to you and hide an extra set.
7. Avoid getting blocked in the driveway; keep the door unlocked for a quick escape. Keep the fuel full at all times.
8. Open a separate bank account.
9. Keep important documents (license, credit cards, bank information) and phone numbers in a safe place.

Once I moved completely away and out of the abusive relationship, I had actions to take before I could start rebuilding my life. I would make a decision to:

1. File a restraining order at the local city county building and keep it on my person at all times.
2. Let a close friend or family know a restraining order is in place.
3. Inform the children's school and caregivers. Explain the situation; give them a copy of the order.
4. Change locks. Or find a place to stay.
5. Change your routine pattern, and day-to-day activities.
6. Rent a post office box for separate mail and packages.
7. Seek help from a therapist and monitor my childrens grades at school.
8. Gain empowerment. Get strong, trust my decisions, and recognize my talents and push forward.
9. Therapy and group counseling I found were very powerful tools for my growth.
10. The past is the past, stand on it and rise above it.

"Un-forgiveness denies the victim the possibility of parole and leaves them stuck in the prison of what was, incarcerating them in their trauma and relinquishing the chance to escape beyond the pain."
TD Jakes

Chapter 12
Escape

The overwhelming feeling I have at this moment is one of release, unspeakable peace, divine balance and harmony.

I see it.

No more darkness. No more burdens. Not in the sense I have known them.

For God has revealed to me an avenue to freedom. And it has been there all along.

My heart shall no longer be dismayed.

My burdens I place at Jesus's feet to stay and to lay.

No longer am I obstructed.

My mind is free and clear by letting go of someone I thought was so dear.

I had to reevaluate and reposition, Stop, stand and listen to my inner voice – the one You gave to me: the one that sings of strength, power and the choice most Divine.

I now walk the proper path, I'm wearing a brand new pair of shoes...

Maya Angelou said it best,
"My mission in life is not merely to
survive, but to thrive; and to do so
with some passion, some compassion,
some humor, and some style."

"My Relationship with Mom"
Part two of English paper—Jade

After reading Mom's diary, I started feeling life was really a mask. The very idea of going through the motions of everyday living and only being able to peep in on a fraction of what really goes on in people's lives is in its own way a form of `blankness'; and what we become to each other behind that: not knowing what's really going in each other's lives – it's got us cheating ourselves.

We become partial to each other. In the sense, we become only fractions of who we are and the only thing worth judging, I know, for a fact, is a whole: The whole of somebody. That's how I discovered what my mom and I needed to start doing: The both of us needed to start filling that "whole. I am now able to move forward and express compassion for my mother.

My mom and I have been through a whole lot the past nineteen years, but last year when she divorced my father, around the beginning of November, we started growing close. We became so close I started being exactly who I am around her and noticed she was doing the same around me.

There aren't any masks anymore. I started realizing in my way I was dressing up, too. I can reveal to her, now, my deepest darkest secrets, knowing she too can reveal hers to me. It's not dark at all, light now flows between us, not obstructed by anything but our love which is how it should be. Because no matter what: Love is not an obstruction.

Now she's different. She has transformed. She's brighter, more confident, and more secure. Her smiles are real. She's relaxed, in a way somebody can only be, when they're free, free of the things that once weighted on their wings.

My mother is flying now. And I'm holding her hand. I think I see where she wants to take me, and I feel thankful and blessed I have someone with her strength and power to endure standing alongside me, rooting for me to succeed.

If We Can Mend Our Broken Relationship So Can You. Forgive and Let Go!

Epilogue

To my dissatisfaction divorce was not an option but inevitable. I had to change within in order to change my outcome. In order for me to blossom I had to forgive. While still in the abusive marriage, working, taking care of children, and a Sunday school teacher, I planted a seed and watered each assignment. I overcame the dark years, escaped and completed a four-year Bachelor of Science in Business Management.

I'm becoming the person I always wanted to be, mentor to young people, a promotional model, real estate broker, inspirational speaker and author. I'm not a prisoner anymore but a flight attendant traveling the world, capturing every moment. My daughter is entering her final year in the Full Sail University Graphic Designer program and started her own cleaning service called Charismatic Cleaning.

To my daughter and the daughters across the world, you are valuable, respectable and indispensable. Don't become bitter and harden your heart. Forgive. Have a Daffodil heart.

Capture the moment and take on the enormous pleasures of a mother daughter relationship. The evidence throughout this book expresses that our destiny in life sometimes comes unexpectedly through events we never expected.

Even though we thought we made the best choices for our life, our choices may come as scars of the reality of love. However, I want all to know I'm delivered and made whole. I stand on solid ground. No need to worry. My love for my children and myself is greater than any earthly man. "Challenges make you discover things about yourself that you never really knew. They're what make the instrument stretch - what make you go beyond the norm." Cicely Tyson. Greater things are yet to come.

BEWARE OF THE SIGNS

Clear signs an abuser is not changing:

1. He's in denial; nothing is wrong in the relationship when abuse took place.
2. He minimizes the abuse or down plays the seriousness of it.
3. He takes no ownership for his actions and/or blames others for his behavior.
4. He reverses roles and convinces you you're abusive and the root cause.
5. He pressures and makes you think counseling is the cure all.
6. He guilt trips you into giving him another chance (ie. You pity me don't you.).
7. He says you've invested too many years in the relationship to just throw it away.
8. He has mood swings (ie. Dr. Jekyll and Mr. Hyde)
9. He plays the children against you.
10. He says he can't get the help he needs unless you stay.
11. He continually displays jealousy and controlling behavior
12. He seeks sympathy from not only you, but your children, family members and friends (manipulates the trust).

Appendix

The Daffodil Plan of Forgiveness is the process and action of letting go the vengeful spirit, releasing of hurt, painful events and negative thoughts.

De'Metria Hayes

DAFFODIL

While working collaboratively on the artwork for the book, my daughter Charisma and I realized we needed a title that would reflect the tonal resonance of our covers art, as well as thematically appropriate.

"Forgiveness" was one of many we considered. But, after much research, I thought "Forgiveness" might be to bold and wanted to use a softer and more inviting title.

I prayed about it, meditated and spoke to friends and family to get their opinion. In my search, for the best title for this book that for a title that expresses the power of a mother-daughter bond I discovered spiritual meanings of several beautiful flowers: the Amaryllis, Apple Blossoms, Bird of Paradise, and Daffodils.

In my excitement, I shared my discovery with my daughter. I told her that the Amaryllis Flower signifies success won after a struggle; that Apple Blossoms represent peace and love; the Bird of Paradise symbolize freedom, good perspective, and faithfulness.

However, I was looking for a title that expressed the sheer power of a mother-daughter bond and none of these flowers seemed to fit. Until the day I happened upon the flower Daffodil.

I learned that Daffodils signify a burst of expression, sunshine, and a ray of hope. Daffodils symbolize faith, honesty, truth, love, forgiveness, and especially a new beginning.

"Why not call it that," my daughter said.

Blueberry Prayer

The Blueberry Prayer holds the symbolic meaning of strength, positivity, peacefulness, calmness, serenity, and dignity and being uplifted.

The Meaning of the Colors on the Cover Page

The cover's artwork is a reflection of a mother's love. The color combined represents strength, energy and love, clarity of awareness, confidence and faith and the willingness to fight. Pink symbolizes calm, newness and pure love.

Orange combines the energy of red and the happiness of yellow. Yellow represents clarity of awareness, joy and happiness. Blue represents communication, trust, tranquility, peace, harmony, confidence and faith.

Red represents conflict, strength, energy, power, determination as well as passion, desire, and love. Green represents renewal, self-respect and well-being, growth, healing and freshness. Purple represents purpose, dignity, independence, creativity, and brings peace of mind.

Acknowledgments

To my mom, Sheridan Johnson Williams, I am grateful for you believing in me. You said when I get tired of this I would leave. You had faith I would wake up, remove the blinders from my eyes and get out of the abusive relationship that overtook me, when many others didn't.

To my family, pops', aunts, uncles, nieces, nephews and cousins (you know who you are) too many to name, thank you for all your support and encouragement. My siblings, you didn't always know what to do but the love and prayers covered me. My fellow flight attendants and pilots, thank you for your help with misspelled words and marketing tips.

My children who are my world and the love of my life, Charisma, Christian, and Christopher enduring the long nights at the computer, papers scattered and the odd times of day and night I write.

To my sister's-in-law and brother's -in-law to which this union separated us, I dearly love and have a special place in my heart for you.

Words cannot express my gratitude to Editor Tina Winograd, JR Lankford, journalist Kiyana Wilkins and Regina Johnson for their professional advice and assistance in polishing this manuscript.

I want to thank Graphic Designer Charisma Stirgus for her skills and contribution in designing the front and back cover. Samir Johnson for the author photo and his contribution with the making of Daffodil booktrailer.

About the Author

DeMetria Hayes the mother of three children. She is a Detroit, Michigan native currently living in Durham, NC. She is a proud University of Phoenix Bachelor of Science business degree graduate. She grew up quiet and shy but engaged in every after school and summer school program she could. She loved the world of education and wanted to absorb all she could. She is an Author, Motivational Speaker, Flight Attendant and mentor's young adults.

———

The story behind Daffodil: Growing up I had to get my thoughts down by my own hand— I captured the event, or moment, writing what I heard or saw on a napkin, a piece of tissue, anything I could find. An electrifying surge of energy stimulates my mind and body down to my fingers as the pen glides across the paper. Writing is like oil to the engine for me; I can't image life without it.

Through my writing, I wanted to inspire and motivate my daughters, who I couldn't reach. I needed to find a way to mend our relationship. So I chose to complete and publish my first book, "Daffodil" A Mother's Journey, dedicated to her. Writing this book was the only way I could express to her what I couldn't say out loud. She is an extension of me, and I am honored to be her mother.

Important Information
You should keep on hand

Police Station#

Doctor#

Medication

Emergency number:

1.

2.

3.

STEP 1 - It starts with your emergency plan

STEP 2 – Make sure you have important contact numbers, documents and medicine together

STEP 3 – Determine who needs to know the plan?

STEP 4 – Plan, write it down, and then execute them

STEP 5 – Keep your plan in a safe location

Statistics/Facts

According to the U.S. Department of Justice, between 1998 and 2002:

Of the almost 3.5 million violent crimes committed against family members, forty-nine percent of these were crimes against spouses. Fifty percent of offenders in state prison for spousal abuse had killed their victims.

In 2000, 1,247 women and 440 men were killed by an intimate partner. In recent years, Approximately 1.3 million women and 835,000 men are physically assaulted by an intimate partner annually in the United States.

Ninety-two percent of women who were physically abused by their partners did not discuss these incidents with their physicians; fifty-seven percent did not discuss the incidents with anyone.

Battered women are not the only victims of abuse - it is estimated that anywhere between 3.3 million and 10 million children witness domestic violence annually. Research demonstrates that exposure to violence can have serious negative effects on children's development.

Sharmila Lawrence, National Center for Children in Poverty, Domestic Violence and Welfare Policy: *Research Findings That Can Inform Policies on Marriage and Child Well-Being* 5 (2002).

Matthew R. Durose et al., U.S. Dep't of Just., NCJ 207846, *Bureau of Justice Statistics, Family Violence Statistics: Including Statistics on Strangers and Acquaintances, at 31-32 (2005)*, http://www.ojp.usdoj.gov/bjs/pub/pdf/fvs.pdf

Resources

Where to go for help when needed: A Domestic Violence or Abuse shelter or crisis centers:

Toll Free Hot Lines:

In the United States: National Domestic Violence Hotline at 800-799- (SAFE) 800-799-7233
National Sexual Assault Hotline -- (800) 656-HOPE

Stalking Resource Center -- 1-800-FYI-CALL

Web address: Worldwide International Directory:

www.ncadv.org
www.womenslaw.org
www.womenshealth.gov

Thank you for taking the time to read
"Daffoil" Mother's Journey

Please show your support by writing a review
and hit "like" my daffodil Facebook page.
If you're looking for a motivational speaker for
your next conference or event please contact
me:

Web address: www.demetriahayes.com or

Email address: daffodil@demetriahayes.com

Twitter @demetriahayes

Instagram: daffodil_demetriahayes